STEVE GREENHALGH was born in Oldham. In February 1974 he was appointed as an RSPCA inspector for the Lancashire East area and worked there for twenty-eight years. As well as writing this memoir of those years, Steve has written a work of non-fiction, a children's book, *The Wars of the Weevils*, and several volumes of poetry. Steve is also a songwriter and a member of a band, The Yuve.

# A SEAL PUP IN MY BATH

Steve Greenhalgh

Constable • London

Constable & Robinson Ltd
3 The Lanchesters
162 Fulham Palace Road
London W6 9ER
www.constablerobinson.com

First published in the UK by Constable,
an imprint of Constable & Robinson Ltd., 2011

A copy of the British Library Cataloguing in
Publication data is available from the British Library

ISBN 978-1-84901-339-0

Printed and bound in the EU

1 3 5 7 9 10 8 6 4 2

*For my wife Kathie and our daughter Emma Kate,*
*without whose help this would not have been possible.*

*Thanks to Mike and Margo Goodenough,*
*John and Alice Cooper, and Krystyna Green*
*for their invaluable assistance.*

# ONE

'Wow! It's perfect for Rolf. We'll get the film crew round there straight away.'

The scene was the RSPCA call centre for the north-west and one of the controllers answering the phones had just informed the BBC production team of a rescue job about to be tasked to the Lancashire East inspector – me.

The BBC hit programme *Animal Hospital* was being recorded in the region and a film crew was stationed at the call centre near Manchester ready to respond to any calls that might fit their bill. The legendary, much loved Rolf Harris fronted the show – a man of many talents and, unusually, a master of them all. The programme had proved immensely popular with the public and had showcased the work of the Society over many years.

Personally, when I heard that the BBC would be filming in the area I had some misgivings about the whole thing. Till then, as a rule, I had always got the job done before involving any media folk. It was a policy that had served

1

me well in the past but would have to be abandoned now: I had to change my ways whether I liked it or not. My only hope was that nothing of interest would happen in my patch while the film crew was in town. That phone call blew my hopes out of the water and, inevitably, the rescue itself turned out to be awkward and out of the ordinary.

I asked for assistance, and was delighted when Inspector Sue Clough came down from north Lancashire to help. It just so happens that Sue, in addition to her excellent qualities as an RSPCA inspector, is a stunningly beautiful lass and I hoped that the camera would naturally follow her rather than myself on our rescue mission.

A marooned cat had been sighted clinging to the branches of a large bush a few feet above the gloomy waters of the Leeds & Liverpool canal at Nelson, in the Pendle area north of Burnley. It was a cold winter's day and I was in Darwen when the call came through. I estimated I'd reach Nelson in about twenty minutes and arranged to meet Sue there. This was all to the good as we'd have half an hour or so to assess the situation before the film crew arrived.

Mrs Sutton, the caller, lived in a quiet little street adjoining the canal near one of the many small bridges that straddled it. Unfortunately, there was a mix-up over the bridge number and I met Sue at the wrong one. We started walking along the towpath towards the centre of Nelson, looking out for the cat along the way.

'It must be here!' I said. 'They said the location was close to the bridge.' I was finding it difficult to match up the information on my job sheet with what we were seeing.

Sue stopped and shook her head. 'Something's not right.' She suggested we ring the caller. A few minutes later the mix-up over bridge numbers was resolved and we were knocking on Mrs Sutton's door.

'Come in. My name's Nellie. Sit thee down.' Inside, tea and home-made oat and honey biscuits were on the table waiting for us. We really wanted to get on with the job but Nellie said she had more to tell us and the biscuits looked delicious. Just then, a young lad about ten years old knocked on the door and ran into the house.

'Ah, Jimmy!'

Our host explained that the youngster had seen the trapped cat about an hour ago and had called to tell her. It was well known in the neighbourhood that she was fond of animals, and she had more than a few of her own. In fact, a great big friendly ginger and white tomcat had parked itself in Sue's lap and two perky little Yorkshire terriers were romping around my feet craving attention.

'Do you think the cat is hurt or injured, Jimmy?' I asked.

'I don't think so, mister. Just cold and frightened.'

'Jimmy's a good lad,' said Nellie. 'He's always lookin' out for the animals. Will you show the officers where the cat is, Jimmy?'

'Aye, missus.'

Nellie reached into her apron pocket and retrieved a twenty-pence piece which she pressed into the young lad's outstretched hand. 'Goodness will always be rewarded in this house and don't you forget that, Jimmy.'

Jimmy thanked her, and the four of us set off up the

road towards a narrow bridge across the canal. A short distance along the towpath Jimmy pointed to a bush growing out of the water near a high wall on the far side and we saw the black and white cat huddled uncomfortably in its branches. He looked thoroughly miserable, shivering with cold and fright.

Sue and I walked round and considered the possibility of reaching down over the wall to rescue the animal. The sheer drop to the water was around twenty feet and not much less to the cat. What was more, the branches of a tree seemed an impossible barrier to such an approach. I leaned forward over the edge of the wall, just to make sure, and nearly lost my footing.

'Blimey, Steve!' yelled Sue. 'You frightened me to death.'

'Sorry. Still, it would have been a laugh for the spectators.' There were folk everywhere, and a posse of Jimmy's friends had joined him and Nellie Sutton on the bridge. Like us, they were wondering what would happen next.

'I think we'd better try to get the boat up from Manchester,' I suggested.

'Best bet, I should say,' Sue agreed. Within a few minutes I'd got through to the call centre to enquire after the boat, but unluckily it was undergoing repairs and a non-starter as far as the rescue was concerned. Sue and I looked at one another and raised our eyebrows. Things were going badly, and were about to get worse. The film crew arrived.

Their leading light was athletic looking and wore jeans and a designer sweater. He had a light raincoat over his shoulders and was smiling as he approached us.

'We got here as fast as we could,' he assured us. 'Not missed anything, have we?' Sue looked across at me, obviously recalling my balancing act above the murky waters of the canal.

'Not a lot,' she said, much to my relief.

'What's the plan then?' he enquired. I thought for a minute.

'I think it's time to call the fire brigade. We'll see where we go from there.'

That was it. Cameras and other essential equipment were quickly in place and the *Animal Hospital* team did a short interview with me while their leader stood some distance away chatting to Sue. The fire brigade arrived in no time and had a look for themselves before joining us.

'It's a tricky one is this,' the officer in charge told me. 'I'm not sure how we can help. Any ideas?'

'We were hoping you'd have some.'

'We've ladders, ropes and cutting equipment, but nothing that seems to fit the bill. I reckon you need a boat.'

'We tried to get ours from Manchester, but it's out of action,' I said.

'Do you know anyone we might approach to borrow one?' I asked. The fireman scratched his head.

'You could try the waterways authority. They certainly have some.'

We retired to Nellie Sutton's house where I spent a good half-hour on the phone. Finally, when all seemed lost, I got an offer of a small rowboat which would arrive by lorry within the hour. It would have to do.

We returned to the canal bank in the hope that a passing

narrow boat might appear on the horizon – not likely in the middle of winter. The crowd had increased threefold and we were the centre of attention, along with the film crew. We had another confab with the fire lads, who told us they would stay around in case they could help out when the boat arrived – providing there were no emergency calls in the meantime.

'Right, lads.' We turned round and there was Nellie Sutton with three of the youngsters who were her eyes and ears in the neighbourhood. They were carrying trays loaded with hot mugs of tea and sandwiches and carrot cake on delicate porcelain plates that looked as if they might have been inherited from her grandmother – far too good for general use.

'You're a life-saver, Mrs Sutton,' I told her, taking a mug of tea off her tray.

'Don't be daft. And call me Nellie, won't you.' I nodded, and waited while Sue grabbed a mug of tea and a slice of carrot cake. Leaving the rest for the film crew and the firemen, we sat down on a couple of plastic bags to enjoy our unexpected elevenses.

'Doesn't seem right sitting here,' she said, 'supping tea and scoffing cake while that poor beggar's stuck there shivering.'

'Too right. And the natives are getting restless.'

'Not to mention the film crew. Eddie thought they'd be finished and on their way by now.' I smiled. 'What's up with you then?' she demanded.

'Eddie, is it? Is he the bloke wearing jeans and a flash sweater?'

'He might be.'

'You've got a boyfriend, haven't you?'

'Not any more. We broke up.'

'Sorry. I didn't know. I thought . . .'

'Four years we were together. Then he ups and dumps me.'

'Must be bonkers,' I said.

'Thanks . . . I think.'

'Went off with another woman, did he?'

'Yes . . . Eddie's wife! That's what we were talking about.' Suddenly, I felt rather ashamed of myself. I had jumped to conclusions seeing them together and, on top of that, it was really none of my business anyway.

'Hey, I feel awful . . .' I began.

'Don't. It's history now.' We sat and finished our tea. It wasn't until I got up to go that I noticed what looked like a tear rolling slowly down her cheek as she stared wistfully into the distance.

The lorry with the rowboat arrived and with the help of the fire lads it was unloaded and carried over to the tow-path ready for launching. I got my van while Sue prepared the boat. I selected two life jackets, a cat basket, a blanket and my grasper from the equipment stored in the back. A grasper is a hollow metal rod about three feet long with a smooth, thick piece of rope threaded through it to form a loop at the end. It's a useful and, if you know what you're doing, perfectly humane means of controlling a feral or frightened animal until it can be confined safely. I arrived back at the boat to be confronted with another problem.

'Hi, Steve,' said Sue, laughing.

'Something wrong?'

'Sort of.'

'Go on then.' The firemen and the film crew were giggling intermittently, which didn't bode well. Finally, Sue enlightened me.

'There's only one oar.'

'What?'

'One oar!'

'Well . . . we'll just have to take turns, then. It should give Rolf and the viewers a laugh if nothing else.'

'It'll look fine after editing,' Eddie said.

'I'll believe that when I see it.'

Sue and I, wearing our life jackets, scrambled into the boat with all our stuff. I took the oar first and paddled a few strokes before handing it over to Sue, who followed suit then passed it back to me. In this Laurel and Hardy fashion we almost managed a straight course towards the cat, still clinging to the bush near the canal wall. The petrified animal was clearly alarmed by our approach but seemed to be in a state of shock, not knowing quite what to do. More than once he looked as though he was about to jump, but had second thoughts. His hesitation allowed Sue to reach out and grab him gently by the scruff of the neck.

'Open the basket, Steve. Quick as you like.' That proved far from easy in the crowded little boat, but somehow I managed it. As the cold, frightened cat was secured the spectators began clapping and cheering. They kept it up as, elated and excited, we paddled our crazy way back to the towpath using our one oar. It was almost surreal, as though we were actors on a stage giving a crowd-pleasing performance without realizing it.

We reached the bank and one of the firemen took the basket off me while Sue jumped out and I passed the rest of the equipment over to her. As I stepped out of the boat I was suddenly aware that the *Animal Hospital* film crew was recording everything. Concentrating solely on the rescue I'd forgotten all about them. It was just as well: if you constantly have one eye on the camera you usually come unstuck and end up looking foolish.

We thanked the fire lads and waved goodbye to Nellie and her helpers before heading for the local animal shelter. Once we were inside the little office we took the young black and white cat out of the basket. He was about two years old, in good condition and obviously used to humans, since he immediately started purring and rubbing his head against the nearest arm or hand he could find.

'Someone will be missing him,' Sue said.

'No ID though,' I commented. 'We'll have to wait and see if they come forward.'

'Let's call him Ben,' she mused. Warming up and feeling more confident, our new friend tucked into a meal and a bowl of milk. To see him safe, sound and relatively happy again was the reward for everyone's efforts. Best of all, Nellie Sutton organized all her youngsters and sent them round the neighbourhood in small groups enquiring after the owner of Ben, and within a day or two she was located.

I was having a late tea one evening and watching an episode of *Animal Hospital* with my wife Kathie when Rolf mentioned the rescue of a cat stuck in a bush above a canal in Nelson. We interrupted our meal to watch the report.

'Hey, we shouldn't bother with this,' I said. 'It'll show Sue Clough and me rowing a boat with only one oar between us. We'll be a laughing stock.'

'Don't be soft,' Kathie replied. 'They'll make you look good. Better than you deserve, I wouldn't be surprised.'

'Thanks!' But Kathie was right. Sue and I looked determined, calm and assured, due to the excellent, painstaking editing. What was particularly stunning was the movement of the rowboat across the water. All the ridiculous swapping of the single oar and the weaving about had been eliminated. There were great shots of Nellie and the cheering crowd on the bridge – number 141 if I remember. I looked a right prune as usual but no amount of editing could put that right.

After showing the rescue itself Rolf announced that the owner of the trapped cat had been found and promptly joined her and 'Ben', as we knew him, on a sofa in the studio. Apparently, her pet had been missing for eleven days in all and his name was actually Matthew. She'd almost given up hope of finding him and was overjoyed to see him again. I always told people not to give up on lost or missing cats, as they occasionally turn up weeks, even months, afterwards. I even heard of one returning home a year after last being seen there. Where it had been all that time was a mystery.

Matthew's owner was happy to have him back, Sue and I were pleased to have pulled off a tricky rescue and Rolf and co. at *Animal Hospital* had a good story for the show. Perfect, really.

One thing still puzzled me, though. I instigated a thorough search of the canal area with the help of Nellie Sutton and her young friends – but the missing oar was never found.

When the *Animal Hospital* series came to an end a party was arranged for everyone connected with the programme. Sadly, I was ill that evening, but Sue Clough kindly took along my daughter's *Rolf on Saturday OK?* LP and asked the great man himself to sign it for her (all right, for me too). Not only did he take time out to oblige, inscribing the song sheet inside 'To EMMA with love, Rolf Harris', he also drew a caricature of himself beside the lyrics of 'The Laughing Policeman'. A true gent indeed.

# TWO

On a bitterly cold winter's evening, as hailstones clattered against the windows, Kathie and I huddled round the small open fire in our half-empty living room. Beneath our feet the layers of industrial-strength brown paper that served as a carpet rustled at the slightest movement. The house was not centrally heated, but we could not close the door to keep the heat in because, like all the others, the handle had been removed by the previous tenant and it would be impossible to open it again. A glaring light emanated from the bare light bulb in the middle of the ceiling. In fact, there wasn't a light shade left in the whole place nor a plug still remaining in bath, basin or sink. It was our second week in the Society's tied house and there was no doubt that the spartan living conditions were tempering the elation of starting out upon my new career as an RSPCA inspector and our wedding the month before.

'Tell me again,' mused Kathie. 'How did we end up living here – like this?

'I'm sorry . . . I think we've just been unlucky with the house. I've got estimates for the repairs and we'll laugh about it one day. Wait and see.' I looked across at her smooth beautiful face glowing in the firelight and leaned forward to kiss her cheek gently. 'Don't worry. It won't always be like this. Promise.' She smiled and sipped her coffee. At least that was still piping hot. The minutes passed in silence as we contemplated the fire and the leaping shadows dancing on the bare walls.

'Steve. I just realized. You never answered my question. How did we end up here and like this?'

'That advert, I suppose.'

'Yes. That advert!'

> RSPCA REQUIRES INSPECTORS between 22 and 35 years of age. Candidates should be of good general education and possess a clean full driving licence. Six months intensive training course to be undertaken at the Society's Headquarters and in the field. Applications please to the Training Superintendent by 26 June 1973.

Some nine months ago on my way home one evening I had bought a copy of the *Manchester Evening News* and, unexpectedly, it changed our lives for ever. The prospect of a career in animal welfare had always appealed to me and I wondered why I had never seriously considered the possibility before. A few years back I'd desperately wanted to be a vet but had soon realized that the qualifications and long training period were a step too far for me. With the trimming of my aspirations in that direction I hadn't thought of other possibilities in animal welfare work, despite seeing RSPCA inspectors at the local vet's when I'd taken next door's old collie, Samson, for his annual check-up. His owner, Mrs Barber, had chronic arthritis in her hands and I often ended up exercising the dog or taking him to the vet when occasion demanded, but for some reason I'd never quite made the connection and considered a career with the Society.

Ironically, just the day before buying the paper and seeing the RSPCA advert I had been interviewed by Manchester Education Authority for the post of senior technician in the science department of a large city high school. I'd been sorely tempted to accept the position with its increased salary and holidays when the portly chairman of the interview panel interrupted my thoughts. 'There is, to be fair, something of a fly in the ointment, Mr Greenhalgh.'

'Oh?' I waited with bated breath, unable to imagine what could possibly be the problem.

'Harpurhey, I'm afraid, is an all girls school. Do you think you'd be able to cope?'

Somehow suppressing my surprise and delight, I looked him straight in the eye.

'It wouldn't be an issue for me,' I assured him. Visions of lovelorn gazes, unremitting feminine adulation and enough Valentine cards to decorate a mansion drifted before my mind's eye. I told the chairman I'd think it over and let them know within forty-eight hours. Then came the RSPCA ad, and knowing without question that I would accept that job if I were fortunate enough to be offered it I reluctantly turned down the position at Harpurhey High School – but not without a lump the size of a golf ball in my throat.

It was some two weeks later that I was invited down to RSPCA Headquarters to appear before a selection committee and, if successful, undergo a full medical examination by the Society's doctor. Unknown to me then, there had been almost three thousand applications for the posts and I was one of the sixty lucky individuals who'd made it through to the interview stage. As there were only twenty or so places available on the training course I needed to be a little luckier yet.

'We could make a short holiday out of the trip,' said Kathie. We'd been going out together for three and a half years and were saving for a deposit on a house. 'Borrow your friend Andy's tent. Roughing it for a few days would be fun.'

'Hm. We'd need the sleeping bags and stove too.'

'Do you remember how to put that tent up?'

'No. But I know it comes down a lot faster than it goes up. I don't fancy backpacking and train journeys, to be honest.'

'We could hire a car,' she suggested. 'I get paid at the end of the week.'

'Great idea!'

And, of course, it was. If only I'd listened to Kathie and

hired a car for the journey everything would have been all right. But I thought about our holidays to come in August and weekend trips out. Stupidly, I decided to buy one instead.

Scanning the endless columns of *Vehicles For Sale* I picked out an old Austin A40 that seemed to fit the bill. At the sale address I was greeted by a long-faced youth with acute halitosis who described the car in glowing terms. Nevertheless, I insisted on a test drive, and when he saw that I meant business the colour noticeably drained from his cheeks. He stood well back as I started the engine – at the sixth attempt – and pulled away from the kerb in a cloud of smoke.

Despite my initial reservations I was surprisingly impressed with my charge until I tried to steer round a sharp right-hand bend. Approaching cautiously, I turned the wheel, naturally expecting an appropriate response from the old Austin. Nothing much happened. The little A40 turned out to have a turning circle akin to the *Titanic*'s. Luckily I was only going 20 mph and managed to negotiate the bend in time and intact. Leaving the car where it was I walked back white faced and informed the sheepish-looking owner, from a distance, that the deal was off.

The next car I pinpointed was a white-roofed, maroon Ford Anglia, registration number HN 2713, mine for a mere fifty quid. (Why is it so much easier to recall long redundant car registrations than it is to remember anniversaries and birthdays?) I was hardly an expert when it came to judging second-hand motors, and the fact that it started first time and nothing fell off during the obligatory test drive was enough to persuade me to part with my money.

Unduly pleased with myself I drove straight round to Kathie's to show off our new wheels, which she examined with a barely concealed look of horror on her face.

'What's all that blue smoke coming out of the exhaust?' she enquired.

'Don't worry. That's normal for an older car,' I assured her. Moving on, she began to wind down the passenger window, which promptly dropped out of view in a blur of smeared glass. 'No problem . . . I'll fix that easily enough.'

'These doors are too heavy for their hinges. There's a two-inch gap at the top. I can hardly shut the passenger door at all.'

'Well,' I reasoned, 'we can both use the driver's side, can't we? Be fair . . . you can't expect a Rolls-Royce for fifty quid.'

With the transport sorted – to my satisfaction at least – I requisitioned Andy's tent and equipment and bought a decent up-to-date road map in preparation for the journey down south. I arranged for a quick trim of my long hair and late that evening we were waved off by my parents. In the broken mirror I could see Dad shaking his head as the Anglia's old engine roared like a lion with colic as we pulled away.

Miraculously, nearly 300 trouble-free miles later, we arrived safely at our campsite on the outskirts of a still sleepy Sussex town and pitched our borrowed tent in the early dawn light. Kathie was wearing my ex-army combat jacket, which left little of her slight, delicate figure visible.

She hit her thumb with the rubber hammer whilst knocking in a tent peg and barely stifled a scream. I tripped over a rope and established intimate contact with a cow pat. Laughing, we rubbed noses like Eskimos (something we'd always done) and made huge mugs of tea before the stove coughed and spluttered to empty. None of it seemed to matter as we looked out from our newly erected refuge at a magnificent sunrise over the dew-ridden Downs. Then, perhaps more tired than we realized, we keeled over asleep on top of our sleeping bags on the floor of the tent.

At 9.58 a.m. precisely, feeble and exhausted, I arrived outside RSPCA headquarters, an imposing manor house in extensive lawned grounds off a quiet lane near the centre of Horsham, a busy Sussex market town which still retained an air of timeless, genteel prosperity.

Two minutes later and right on time I was announcing myself at the reception desk when, suddenly, all hell broke loose. Fire alarms throughout the place trilled loudly in unison and people came hurrying out of a multitude of rooms and corridors before surging outdoors to predetermined locations at the front and rear of the building.

Unaffected, the elegant receptionist studied the list below her desk before announcing confidently, 'Ah, Stephen Greenhall—'

'Greenhalgh,' I corrected. 'It's pronounced halsh. The last two syllables sound as if you're telling someone to be quiet in a library.'

'Really? Well, that's as may be. But you should already be at point F2, middle of the lawn at the back. Opposite

the windows of the legal superintendent's department. Go
on . . . hurry!'

'What about you?' I enquired.

'Oh, I'm coordinating here. It's only a test. My colleague,
Sheila, set the alarms off in the back room.'

'Well, if it's only a test, I'll be okay to stay, eh?'

'F2, Mr Greenbank. F2!' Her pointing finger ultimately
proved irresistible. Grinning, I strolled nonchalantly round
the side of the building to point F2, where a chattering
crowd had already gathered. As I waited my eyes widened
and I began to stare open mouthed, amazed at the sheer
number of people constantly adding to the size of the
throng. The old place was clearly something of a Tardis.
I almost expected Jon Pertwee to arrive in a red velvet
jacket – though that said, some of the shirts on display
would have given his ruffles a run for their money.

Everything quickly returned to normal and before long
I found myself seated in a narrow corridor with a clutch of
other prospective candidates for places on the inspectorate training course. As is always the case in such situations,
they all seemed smarter, better groomed and altogether
more suited to be chosen than I was. Despair and a certain
sense of déjà vu were beginning to loom when, unexpectedly, the broad thick-set chap with a dark moustache who
was sitting along from me spoke up. 'Had far to come?'

'Manchester,' I replied hopefully, fairly confident he'd
have heard of it despite his strong cockney accent. He
scratched his head and paused theatrically.

'Just up the motorway from Watford, isn't it?'

'I deserved that, I suppose.' We laughed and introduced ourselves. Marvin Lampton turned out to be an Eastender and ran a pub to boot. He had a wry sense of humour and, it transpired, a talent for playing the banjo.

'I don't fancy our chances today,' he whispered.

'Why not?'

'I hear the rest are all ex-military or police – used to discipline and a uniform, good at taking orders and all that. We don't seem to fit the bill.'

'I used to be in the Scouts,' I recalled.

'Oh. That's all right then.'

Marvin's name was called and he gave a thumbs-up sign as he departed for the interview room. Some fifteen minutes later he emerged, smiling and upbeat.

'It went well then?'

He nodded. 'Want some good advice, Steve?'

'Of course.'

'Make them laugh. Make 'em giggle, my son!'

'What . . . tell jokes?'

'Nah. You know . . . make them smile!'

Inadvertently, as it happened, I did. The interview panel consisted of two men and two women, the men tall, bespectacled and severe, the women manicured, well dressed and almost, but not quite, smiling. During my inquisition I was nervous but managed to exude enough false confidence to answer the questions reasonably positively. Then, suddenly, I was taken aback.

'What experience do you have of handling and caring for animals, Mr Greenhargh?'

I decided to let the mispronunciation pass and racked my brains for a convincing reply. Experience . . . experience . . . ? Resisting the urge to mention my infrequent visits to the vet with Mrs Barber's old collie, I remembered Billie and Peter, the family budgerigars.

'Well, we had a couple of budgies. Not at the same time, though. We had one and then we got another when the first one died.' The suppressed grins threatening to break out on the other side of the table were alarming, but I'd started so I had to finish, as it were. 'I looked after them while Mum was at work – sometimes,' I added lamely. Despite themselves, all four of the panel burst out laughing. Grinning inanely à la Frank Spencer, I could only hope Marvin had been right or my prospects of a place on the forthcoming training course were almost non-existent.

'That's fine,' announced the taller of the two men, quickly recovering his solemnity. 'Could you wait outside, please, and we'll inform you of the result of your application shortly.'

I tottered out to re-join Marvin and the others, and he glanced up enquiringly. 'Did you make them laugh, Steve?'

'Oh, I did that all right,' I assured him. 'I left a bunch of happy hyenas in there.'

'Then you're in! No doubt about it. You've cracked it, my son!'

I did doubt it, though. How could he possibly, conceivably, be right? Still, not ten minutes later, we learned to our delight that both of us had been successful after all. In fact, all that remained before taking our places on the training course were the medical examinations to follow shortly.

With the help of the receptionist's well-meant directions we managed to lose ourselves in the rambling, rabbit warren of a building and the room set aside for the use of the Society's doctor proved to be the proverbial needle in a haystack. Fortunately, a quite gorgeous young secretary in the transport supervisor's office felt sufficiently sorry for us to direct us back onto the right path. Marvin's eyes were on stalks, I noticed, as this vision glided alluringly away down the corridor.

'They don't make 'em like that in London then?' I enquired.

'Only for export.'

'She's okay, but I reckon you can't beat a reet good-lookin' Lancashire lass.'

'Maybe you're right, Steve. Has to be some reason you lot grub for a living up there.'

'Cheers!'

My medical proved relatively straightforward. The Society's doctor was one of the old school, the type that reputedly scorned anaesthetics and operated with a scalpel in one hand and a cigar in the other. I answered the usual stream of curt textbook questions: Height? Five foot nine inches. Weight? Nine stone six pounds. Hair? Yes. Long and light coloured but under orders to become short and light coloured. Previous significant illnesses and ailments? Only (and appropriately) chickenpox. Operations? Tonsils, adenoids and appendix – all removed in childhood.

Smoker? Definitely not. Vegetarian? Afraid not, but maybe one day . . . ad infinitum, it seemed. However, the examination ended at last and I was about to leave when the doctor stroked his chin thoughtfully with his right hand.

'Mr Greenalg . . .'

'Greenhalgh,' I corrected, wearily.

'Hm . . . that's as may be,' he growled, echoing the receptionist earlier. 'How did you get here today?'

'Let's see . . . M6, M1, then Watford, Slough, Windsor . . .'

'Yes, yes. By car then?' Puzzled, I nodded agreement. 'And you drive regularly back home?'

'Yes.'

The doc paused and squeezed his nostrils between the forefinger and thumb of his left hand. 'Then you should be aware that you're a danger, indeed a menace, on the road. Your eyesight must have deteriorated substantially in the, what is it, three years since you were tested. I suggest that you take the train home.'

'But I've never needed glasses before . . . I don't understand . . .'

'Don't worry. It's quite common for someone to think their vision is A1 when it's not. They think the way they see things is the way everyone else does . . . bit like politicians in that respect, I suppose. Otherwise, though, you're fine. My advice is get some goggles asap and you'll never look back. Or, if you do, you'll see things properly, at least.'

Back at the campsite Kathie saw me approaching and

assumed the worst. My glum head-down aspect didn't bode well.

'No luck then?' she enquired sympathetically.

'Oh, I'm on the training course. No problem there.'

'Brilliant! What's with the long face then?'

'It's the medical . . .'

'What's wrong, Steve?'

'Well . . . I've got . . .'

'What?'

'I've got . . .' Somehow, the words stuck in my throat.

'Is it contagious? Am I going to get it too?'

'No. It's just that I've got . . .'

'Not that wretched Hong Kong flu, is it?'

'Will you listen, Kathie? It's serious. I've got . . . to wear glasses!' At last I'd blurted out the dreaded news. There was a short silence that seemed to go on for ever. How she would react dominated my thoughts completely. Would she fancy me any more? Was it the end of the road? Could our love possibly survive specs?

'You idiot!' she cried, hugging me. 'I thought something terrible was wrong. A pair of specs aren't going to wreck our relationship.'

'Are you sure?' One X-rated snog later I was reassured enough to fetch a bottle of Rioja and a Chinese meal back to the tent. During the course of the evening, however, Kathie could see that I was still worried.

'It's cool to wear glasses, Steve.'

'Really? You don't see James Bond wearing them, do

24

you? Unless they're shades, a disguise for a laser weapon or a spy camera or something.'

'Well . . . I think they're cool.'

'Name me one cool person who wears specs, then.' She looked nonplussed for a moment, but then produced a flash of inspiration out of nowhere.

'Peter Fonda. He wears them in *Easy Rider*. He's cool, right?' It was a short straw to clutch at but, rather surprisingly, I slept well that night – aided and abetted by a few more glasses of excellent wine.

The journey home began well enough. Despite the doctor's comments I was (foolishly) determined, taking it very carefully, to get us back in the car. Then, before I did anything else, a trip to Lofthouse's opticians would be a priority. We averaged nearly 40 mph in the noisy, rattling old Anglia until, just north of Oxford, Kathie's voice broke into my thoughts. There was a puzzled expression on her face.

'Steve, what's that red light mean?'

'Where?'

'On the speedo.'

'Oh, that red light. It's been on for ages, but everything seems okay.'

'Shouldn't we get it checked out?' Before I could reply the car began coughing, spluttering and generally having an auto-fit before slowing to an embarrassing halt. We looked across at each other, faces etched with foreboding, as a drizzling rain blurred the view from the windows.

'Are we in the AA, Steve?'

'Don't drink enough.'

'You're in nothing at all, are you?'

'There's the Cheltenham and Gloucester, but I don't suppose they'll be much help at the moment.'

'What's to be done, then?'

'I think I saw a garage just back there. I'll see if there's anyone about who can help.'

A hundred and fifty yards away on the same side of the road was M&M Motors, (Distinctive Cars for the Man of Distinction), a slogan that seemed unnecessarily sexist and market restricting to me. Unfortunately, it transpired that M&M Motors sold cars rather than repaired them. But what cars!

I came across Kenneth Motley, a director of the firm, polishing a sparkling Rolls-Royce Silver Cloud in the neat and tidy showroom. 'Like to buy her?' he asked, more in hope than expectation.

'I'd love to, but the pools win isn't due till next week.'

He sighed like a man who'd heard the same answer, or something similar, all too many times before. 'We give credit.'

'Not to me you wouldn't.'

'Ah, pity. How else can I help then?' I explained our predicament and Kenneth pointed me towards the phone in the office showroom. '*Yellow Pages* is in the right-hand top drawer of the desk. Help yourself.'

I rang round the local garages but no one was willing to come out till morning. I arranged 8.30 a.m. with the cheapest quote and imagined Kathie's response to another night of roughing it. Kenneth popped his head round the door. 'Sorted?'

'Tomorrow morning. Best anyone could do.'

'Where will you spend the night?'

'Would you mind if we set up our tent round the back of the garage? We'll leave everything clean and tidy and pay for the privilege, of course.'

'Why don't you sleep in here?'

'The showroom?'

'The Rolls! The back seats are pretty comfortable. I speak from experience after too many late nights and a tipple or two doing the accounts. I've a couple of blankets you can borrow if you need them.'

'That's superb! You're sure about this?'

'Certain. Lock up when you leave and put the keys through the letter box. Access all areas and that includes the bottom drawer of my desk. The whisky bottle's in there.'

'Hey, thanks! We won't need the blankets as we've got sleeping bags, but the whisky's a different matter. How much do we owe you?'

'No charge. I was looking for a couple of night watch-men anyway.'

Kenneth Motley! What a nice guy, I thought, as I tramped back to get Kathie and our gear. We both agreed that it could have been worse – a lot worse. Kipping in the back of a Rolls-Royce in a warm showroom surrounded by a flock of prestige cars, after a meal of sandwiches washed down by a good malt, was no real hardship.

I was assured of a place on the next inspectorate training course and a sleepy Kathie was huddled in a warm beautiful heap next to me. I felt for the first time that, aggravating Anglias apart, things were shaping up nicely and I'd found my vocation.

# THREE

Class B 1973 of RSPCA trainee inspectors gathered together in the classroom at the Society's Horsham headquarters late in July of that year. We were, at least prospectively, the pick of the bunch, the likeliest of lads, the chosen few – well, the chosen twenty-one as it happened. For all that, we were rather a motley crew of varying ages from vastly different backgrounds but all eager to begin our new careers in animal welfare. With unblinkered enthusiasm and expectations high we wondered what would be first on the agenda . . . a lecture on relevant legislation and important points of law, a talk on veterinary matters perhaps, or maybe a demonstration of expert animal handling by members of the training staff? Then, ominously, a large office trolley was wheeled into the room and thick bundles of faded yellow forms were randomly distributed. Len Flint, the training superintendent, sensed chaos and collared myself and Tom Wilson, ex-Navy from Portsmouth, to make sure everyone got a bundle each. More of Len later.

It transpired that the mountain of forms consisted of 'Standing Orders' familiar to, if not loved by, every inspector in the country. There were over a hundred of them and they all had to be read, digested, acknowledged and signed. It was weary work.

During afternoon coffee break, I loitered too near the open door of the superintendent's office. He had noticed that I'd pushed my still quite long hair behind my ears rather than have it cut short.

'Ah, Mr Greenhalgh, isn't it?'

'Yes. I . . .'

'You've got forty-eight hours to get your hair cut – to my satisfaction not yours. Understood?'

I nodded and groaned inwardly, knowing that this time it really would have to be the full short back and sides.

'By the way . . . how's Oldham? Still raining, I expect.'

Astonished that he knew my home town, I admitted that it had been when I'd left on the Sunday.

'I used to be stationed in Oldham – Werneth, near the fire station,' he volunteered. 'The town was full of mills, chimneys and blighters who couldn't speak the Queen's English.'

I laughed. Len was a Londoner, very sleek and a sharp dresser, who liked to present a tough but sophisticated front to the world. I began to wonder if he'd supported my application as we'd got 'smoky Owdham' in common, because despite his words it was clear he still had a weird sort of affection for the place. Actually, it must have suited him, because old Len himself chain-smoked like a chimney. Many of the coffee breaks he called during class were a woefully thin excuse for Len to retire to his office for a quick drag.

At the end of the first day a bowed-headed, aching-wristed trail of trainees departed for their digs wondering quite what they'd let themselves in for. I was sharing accommodation with Marvin Lampton at Warnham, a neat little village near Horsham. It was an old converted railwayman's cottage, ideal except for the postage-stamp-sized bedrooms and a bathroom that might have seemed cosy to Bilbo Baggins and his hobbit mates. It was owned by Hugh and Tina, young first-time buyers who were both 'something in the City' and commuted into London from the nearby village station. The idea of spending two or three hours on a train five times a week travelling to and from work was completely alien, indeed mind-blowing, to me. Like their neighbours and peers, these two really lived for the weekend.

After our evening meal I studied a copy of the RSPCA annual report. Refreshingly, it described its inspectors as 'frontline men and women, on call round the clock, championing animal welfare'. It suddenly clicked, big time, that I was training to be one of their number and, with the pride, came the realization of heavy responsibility. I would be investigating complaints and preventing cruelty to the animals on my patch. In that respect the buck would stop very firmly with me.

I realized that I had joined a large, historic and complex organization. The Society for the Prevention of Cruelty to Animals was founded back in 1824 in a London coffee house, and was the first animal protection agency in the world. The Reverend Arthur Broome of St Mary's, Bromley, and the MP Richard Martin were amongst its leading lights and it became the 'Royal' Society in 1840 when Queen Victoria acknowledged its good work. At the time it was widely accepted that the owner of an animal had the right to do as they pleased with it, and the Society's mission to promote kindness and prevent cruelty must have seemed eccentric, to say the least. The long tradition of utilizing inspectors began when the Reverend Arthur employed a man named Wheeler in the role. He was soon joined by others who checked London's markets and slaughterhouses, and from such small beginnings the RSPCA grew to operate nationwide. Its headquarters is currently in Southwater near Horsham in Sussex and the organization has a ruling council of twenty-five members elected from the membership as a whole. A chief executive and several directors oversee its many departments based there. A network of some 170 local branches, separately run charities, operates under RSPCA and branch rules throughout England and Wales. There are also many animal welfare establishments, homes, clinics and first-class wildlife centres countrywide. Amazingly, the whole thing's funded purely from charitable donations and legacies without government or lottery aid. Amongst the many headquarters departments, all competing for funds, is the Inspectorate. Not surprisingly, it is regarded by many as of major importance. The public's first contact with the

Society is usually through dealings with an inspector and it is inspectors, not buildings, that prevent cruelty on a day to day basis. In 1974 there were 200 inspectors in all, mostly appointed to the local branches that paid an annual sum to headquarters towards 'their' inspector's upkeep. More responsibility. Would I be value for money, 'up to it' or not?

In those far-off days I was a valued customer of the quaintly named Yorkshire Penny Bank. When I presented a cheque to Hugh and Tina for my first week's board and lodging they split their sides laughing. Clearly, they had never heard of Yorkshire's finest fiscal institution.

'Is this for real,' gasped Hugh, 'or some sort of Monopoly bank?'

'It's your rent. Don't worry. You'll get your money all right.'

'Yes . . . but will it have a toy train or Noddy and Big Ears stamped on the notes?'

Embarrassed, I hastened outdoors to meet Marvin for a pre-arranged evening walk around the village and the surrounding countryside.

'Do you think they'll pass muster – the two women in the class?' he asked, as we meandered down quiet country lanes dotted with highly desirable, ultra-expensive properties. There was money, pots of it, in West Sussex and blimey the local shopkeepers knew it. A simple ham salad sandwich cost three times as much as its superior counterpart up north, and a pint of the dodgy local ale would set you back good and proper. Before coming down I'd been determined not to adopt the 'professional northerner' stereotype southerners would expect, but the generally increased cost of living and the Penny Bank business had needled me.

'Wotcher, Steve . . . Steve!'

'Oh, sorry, mate. I must have been daydreaming. I was well away there. What were you saying?'

'The two women in our class – do you think they'll finish the course?'

'I didn't even know they were on antibiotics.'

'You pillock!'

In silence, but smiling, we walked on till we reached a large house with a long front garden overlooking the village green. It had a fine view of the small but scenic duck pond some fifty yards away – hence the name on the gate: Mallard View. Sitting smugly on top of the five-foot wall at the front was a gorgeous, long-coated ginger kitten, probably around four months old. It showed no alarm at our approach and actually rose and sauntered towards us as we got within a few feet of it. Soon, we were making a right old fuss of our new friend, who was happily rolling over and inviting us to continue as long as we liked.

'Well, what a beauty he is,' exclaimed Marvin. I lifted ginger's tail and examined underneath.

'She is!' I corrected him triumphantly. Marvin looked puzzled and a tad disbelieving.

'I thought all ginger cats were toms.'

It was a common misconception that I'd laboured under

34

myself till a question on TV's *Mastermind* had put me right about it.

'Nah. Ginger is like most other colours of cats in that they can be either sex. But tortoiseshells are always females. You know . . . black, brown and white, or black with brown flecks in the coat.'

'All right, all right. You're beginning to sound like Black's Veterinary Dictionary. Not here two minutes and already you're swotting.' We laughed and continued stroking our appreciative new friend.

'What's on the collar?' wondered Marvin. I could make out *Holly*, *Mallard View* and a phone number on the thin metal plate attached to the shiny, rigid, leather-bound collar.

'She's on home ground then. Come on . . . let's be off.'

We left Holly looking sad eyed and rather forlorn as we headed in the direction of The Cat and Bagpipes – a traditional drinkers' pub on the Crawley road recommended by Tina.

After rather too many pints and a good few packets of Planters' dry roasted peanuts we set off back to our digs – thankful that we'd both been given keys to come back when we liked as long as we didn't disturb the natives. There was no sign of Holly, who we imagined was probably stretched out in a luxurious basket somewhere inside Mallard View by that time.

Over the next week or so Marvin and I encountered the ginger kitten repeatedly on our travels and established a firm friendship with her. As soon as we came in sight Holly would eagerly skip along the length of the front wall into our waiting hands. One overcast day it had been raining hard and knowing how much cats hate the rain we were astounded to see the little kitten waiting to greet us as usual in a pitifully bedraggled state. Marvin used his expensive light overcoat to dry her off while I held an umbrella over them and got a soaking for my trouble. It wasn't long afterwards that Holly wanted to accompany us on our travels and sometimes we had to be cruel to be kind and slip away when her attention was diverted elsewhere.

One Thursday, around seven in the evening, we were passing Mallard View again on our way to the pub. It was warm, slightly humid weather and the cool gathering breeze was welcome after a long day with Len in the classroom studying *The Conveyance of Live Poultry Order 1919* in all its inglorious detail. Though tedious and eventually superseded by later legislation, I have always had an inexplicable soft spot for this fowl Act of Parliament and delighted in entertaining friends and family on occasion by reciting poultry provisions verbatim, including two favourites:

> *No person shall transport poultry on any vessel, aircraft or vehicle unless, in respect of that vessel, aircraft or vehicle (as the case may be) the vessel, aircraft or vehicle is equipped so that any receptacle on it containing poultry can be secured in a way which will prevent the receptacle from shifting as a result of the*

*motion of the vessel, aircraft or vehicle. And If any person fails to do anything required to be done by him by or under any of the provisions of this Order, an officer of the appropriate Minister or an Inspector may, without prejudice to any proceedings for an offence out of such default, do or cause to be done the thing so required to be done.*

Phew! But I digress . . . back to Mallard View. We could see no sign of Holly on the front wall or anywhere else for that matter. Marvin and I looked at each other in surprise; then, suddenly, a baleful mewing echoed loudly above our heads. Our eyes following our ears, as it were, we located Holly at the very top of a forty-foot cherry tree halfway down the narrow garden. She'd no doubt been chasing birds and landed herself high up in the branches without realizing it. Initially, we weren't too concerned, confident that, with quiet encouragement, she'd soon come down and join us. Some twenty minutes or so later we were ready to admit defeat. The ginger kitten remained rooted to her exposed spot on a thin branch at the top of the tree. She seemed to be looking down on us in disappointed bewilderment.

'Perhaps the owner might have more success getting her down,' suggested Marvin. 'Let's knock on the door.'

'Give it a go,' I agreed. There was no reply, but old Marvin had a sudden brainwave.

'The village shop might be open. We should be able to get a tin of cat food to entice her down. I'll nip over – see you soon.' Ten minutes later he reappeared carrying a piece of fillet steak.

'They didn't have any tinned cat food left so I bought the last of their fresh meat.'

'Did you get a bottle of Bolli to wash it down with? Champagne's just the thing, you know.'

'Didn't you hear me? It was all they had left, you northern numpty!'

'Well, don't expect me to sub you in the pub, matey.'

'I've plenty on me, no need to worry. You can keep your money safe in your pockets and your Penny Bank, my son.'

The expensive meat had no effect on young Holly. She was a fixture at the top of the cherry tree and it looked like a job for the fire brigade till Marvin had another brainwave.

'Toss a coin for it then,' he said.

'For what?'

'Who goes up the tree.'

I looked at him and maybe it was my imagination but he looked afraid of the outcome – perhaps more afraid than I was myself. While he tossed the coin I started to climb the cherry tree, ducking and diving amongst the branches as I clambered upward. Halfway up I took a breather and made the cardinal mistake of looking down. It took all my self-control to look away and continue to climb.

'Not much further,' shouted Marvin from below. It still looked a long way to me and inching up the higher, thinner branches was a painfully slow process. Finally, Holly was in sight and I was soon stretching out a hand and grabbing her from her perch. She didn't struggle – just buried her head in the front of my coat and snuggled warmly against me as I got us back to ground.

'You're a hero, Steve!'

'I don't know how I did that,' I said, trying to get my breath back and gulping in air. The click of the garden gate drew our attention and an irate, rather plump lady arrived on the spot. She was the picture of alarm and indignation.

'What's all this? What are you hooligans doing in my garden?'

'It's not what you think,' I began, but she had noticed Holly in my arms.

'Are you cat burglars?' she yelled, meaning, as it were, burglars of cats.

'No . . . no,' stuttered Marvin. 'We've just rescued Holly from the top of that cherry tree. She was stuck and couldn't get down.'

Much to our amazement the plump lady calmed down and began to smile. We assumed it was relief that she was confronting a pair of lamebrains as opposed to hardened criminals intent on purloining her pet. I handed the little kitten over to her owner, who promptly gave her a quick peck on the nose and lowered her gently to the ground. There was a momentary silence you could cut through with a knife as the same thought flashed through both Marvin's and my own mind. He was the first to speak. 'Er . . . Is that a good idea – letting her go just here?'

'Oh, that's all right,' the plump lady assured us, grinning at our scruffy, dishevelled appearance. 'Holly's always chasing birds up that tree. She comes down when she wants to and always before supper time. You needn't have bothered "rescuing" her.' With that, she turned on her heel and hurried indoors.

'Well, I like that,' announced Marvin, not liking it at all. 'Look at the state of us and not a word of thanks, kiss my arse or anything. After rescuing her kitten and all.'

'She didn't seem to think Holly needed rescuing. And she'd know, wouldn't she?'

'I suppose so.'

'Come on . . . let's go for that pint.'

'Yeah . . . Hang on! Where's Holly?' We looked round. Then, above us, we heard more baleful mewing. There, at the very top of the cherry tree, was the little ginger kitten.

It was more than a week later when Marvin and I next passed Mallard View. Holly wasn't on the front wall, so we weren't surprised to see her in the old cherry tree. It was difficult to get a good view of the small ginger ball of fur above us through the tangle of branches. We called out her name but there was no sound or movement, which seemed odd.

'Weird,' said Marvin. We continued to call but still there was no response, and alarm bells began to ring. I found myself rushing down the path and scrambling up the tree like a squirrel with its tail on fire. I could feel the thump of my heart as I almost slipped when a thin branch suddenly snapped as I grabbed at it. Reaching Holly, I was horrified to see that her rigid, leather-bound collar had snagged on a broken limb of the tree and she was hanging helplessly – as limp as a rag doll. I was pretty sure that we were too late as I lifted her gently into my arms.

'What's the score?' yelled Marvin.

'She's in a bad way . . . asphyxiation. Ring the vet in Horsham and organize a taxi.'

Marvin banged on the door; fortunately the plump lady was in. Distraught, she directed him to the phone and Marvin did the rest.

The vet found a heartbeat and told us to wait in reception. 'Think she'll make it, Steve?'

'I . . . I really don't know.' I have to admit having my doubts as we sat there waiting for the verdict. Neither of us said very much, though it soon became clear that Marvin's silence could not wholly be put down to anxiety over Holly. He was so obviously gazing in the direction of one of the veterinary nurses that I felt obliged to poke him in the ribs with my elbow on several occasions because the nurse in question and people waiting to see the vet had clearly noticed. They seemed to find it more or less amusing.

Eventually the vet returned and assured us Holly would be all right, though it had been a close call. The danger of loose rigid collars on cats had been brought home to us as trainee inspectors in the most forceful way. Later, Marvin and I delighted in relating our tale to the training superintendent and, indeed, anyone else who would listen. It felt as if we'd been appointed fully fledged inspectors already and we toasted Holly and our luck in The Cat and Bagpipes that evening.

A few days later a distressingly large bill arrived from

the vet, but that afternoon the class was interrupted by the arrival of Mrs Wingfield-Jones, the plump lady from Mallard View. She wished to thank Trainee Inspectors Greenhalgh and Lampton for saving her kitten's life and did so in front of the whole class. Needless to say, we took some stick from the others for weeks on end. Fortunately for us Mrs Wingfield-Jones took the vet's invoice and was more than happy to settle it herself. Still, the only thing that really mattered was that Holly, minus her rigid tartan collar, had fully recovered and was free to chase up and down Mrs Wingfield-Jones's cherry tree whenever she liked.

The six-month training period for RSPCA inspectors in those days was split into three parts. The first consisted of two months of initial training classes at Horsham headquarters, and the second of a month in the field with each of two experienced chief inspectors where we'd get to discover the difficulties and delights of the job under the guidance of chiefs who'd been there and done most of it before. I say most of it because the job has a way of throwing up new, often bizarre, situations that require innovative thinking and a different approach. With the class approaching the field training period we were all wondering where we'd be stationed. It was the general view that one of the postings at least was likely to be somewhere near home so that we could get back at weekends. Little did we know. Even if Len Flint had been a sadist (and there were a few who inclined to that view) it actually depended on which chiefs were available to take trainees at the time. Matching their areas with our home towns was nearly impossible. In any case, we'd no doubt be on duty most weekends dealing with emergency calls so it wouldn't matter where we were stationed. In the event, I got Stafford and Peterborough under Chief Inspectors Edwards and Goodenough respectively. Neither station was exactly handy for Oldham but Stafford seemed to offer some hope at least.

Before field training we had one more field trip out of Horsham. We'd already learned something about work in the auction markets via a day at Guildford with the chief there. We'd also paid a visit to a Ross poultry factory where we'd witnessed the journey of a live chicken through to its appearance as a packaged product ready for the supermarket shelf in a surprisingly short time. Humane it might be but the process left most of us with a sudden burning desire to go veggie. Still, this new expedition promised to be something special. Indeed, it turned out to be a career-breaker for one of the class, who left the Society the next day.

Reading abattoir was not a pretty sight back then. Not that it wasn't well constructed and kept in a generally clean condition, with the equipment and instruments tested regularly to maintain good working order. It was just that, like all abattoirs, it was an intrinsically depressing place. They are charged with doing society's dirty work, to be neither seen nor heard by the rest of us. Only thought about when it can't be avoided, they nevertheless impinge upon the lives of so many – the meat-eating public, farmers, local authority officials, butchers, slaughtermen, and, of course, the animals that end not only their journey by road or rail there but their life's journey too.

We arrived around 11 a.m. and changed into white boiler suits and donned hard hats before we were allowed to enter the premises. We'd already been told by the training superintendent that each of us would be required to stun an animal prior to slaughter and no excuses would be accepted. A few of the class were unhappy about this and couldn't see the necessity of it but I suppose, realistically, we had to be prepared and knowledgeable on the subject if we were going to visit abattoirs on our patch to inspect, comment and make recommendations concerning the welfare of animals.

We were shown a humane killer gun, which shoots a bolt into the head of an animal to render it unconscious, and given a demonstration of its use before we all had to queue to step up to a raised platform above a narrow restraining pen containing the animal to be slaughtered. When stunned, it collapsed to the floor of the pen, which then fell downwards allowing the animal to slide out to undergo pithing and slaughter. The pithing process utilizes a flexible metal rod which destroys the central nervous system.

None of us was looking forward to our turn and the queue of reluctant trainees formed hesitantly and slowly. Marvin was first in line and I was ninth, behind young Harry Mellor. He was the youngest trainee having just turned twenty-two – beating me by eight months or so. All I knew about him then was that he came from Harrogate in Yorkshire, and owned several horses. All too soon, Harry took his place on the platform and waited till the animal was perfectly positioned below. Then, screwing up his courage, he fired. What happened next was astounding. Before our very eyes, like the victim of some magician's weird trick, Harry disappeared from view in a blur. One moment he was there on the platform, humane killer in hand, the next – gone. The clatter of the floor of the pen being released could be heard and the stunned animal slid into view – along with Harry Mellor, who was covered from head to toe in muck and straw. Much to everyone's relief he sat up clutching his chest but not seriously hurt. He survived with bruised ribs (often more painful than broken ones), a sprained wrist and a truly kaleidoscopic collection of cuts and bruises.

What had actually happened was a freak occurrence, we were told. Harry had fired the gun and the bolt had stuck in the animal's head. Before he could let go of the handle he'd been pulled over into the pen as the animal collapsed and landed on top of it. The rest we'd seen for ourselves. For a bolt to stick like that was rare with well-maintained equipment, but stick it certainly had.

I had hoped the incident might have meant the end of training for the day, but I was told to mount the platform and take my turn. A replacement gun was slapped in my hand and, despite my visions of Harry's grisly resurrection, I knew there was nothing for it but to knuckle down to the task. When I eventually fired the gun and realized that I was still there on the platform, unbloodied as it were, I was totally drained of nervous energy and mightily relieved.

Tottering down, I joined the ranks of those who had survived the experience, where a handshake from Ken Price, our token Aussie, brought me painfully back to reality. Thanks, Ken, but, 'Ouch!'

So ended our abattoir adventure in deepest Berkshire. Later, Marvin made much of the look on my face when young Harry Mellor had disappeared. When they were told, Hugh and Tina were sympathetic – after they'd stopped laughing. That night, I stayed in and wrote a letter to Kathie explaining that I might not complete the training period after all. She wrote back telling me that I bloody well would and not to be so silly. You can't argue with a Lancashire lass. As my father often reminded me, they always know best.

I did carry on, of course (or this book would never have been written), and so did a shaken Harry Mellor, but Graham Johnston from Hampshire didn't. Reading had convinced him that he wasn't, after all, cut out for the Inspectorate. We were down to twenty trainees who were looking forward to field training more than ever.

# FOUR

Field training at my first posting, Stafford in the Midlands, began in October 1973. I caught the early morning train from Manchester Piccadilly and met Ted Edwards, the chief inspector, at Stafford station. Ted was a quiet, reserved countryman type, though I found out later that he could sometimes get riled under pressure. Most of the time, though, he was so laid back he could fall backwards, some would say. He was very attached to his pipe, which he'd often smoke with his window down as we drove along, meaning it was a bit parky in the passenger seat. Strong stuff that tobacco was too and it smelt like the devil's armpit. He spoke with a definite accent, but one which I couldn't place and never got round to asking him about. One thing's for certain – it wasn't Brummy.

Some people are very good at what they do and have years of experience behind them; they're well qualified to pass on their knowledge to anyone willing to learn but, somehow, they can't. I once enrolled on a computer course where the college lecturer obviously knew his stuff, but I understood no more about computers and operating one at the end of the course than I had at the beginning. He had it all up there in his brainbox, but he just couldn't impart his knowledge and expertise to others. Ted was like that. I liked the bloke a lot and got on well with him, but I wasn't inspired and didn't learn a lot in my time at Stafford.

To be fair, the chief did have a relatively quiet area where ten jobs on your sheet was almost unknown and pressure was purely tyre related. The true story was all there in my notebook at the end of my month in Stafford – although it took a more experienced eye than mine to pick it out. When an inspector's notebook regularly features entries along the lines of 'Wash Society's vehicle at base', 'Visit branch secretary (re whatever)', 'Confer (with anyone for any length of time)', 'Collect bedding and leave at shelter' then you can be sure the inspector isn't exactly run off his feet. Incidentally, the notebooks used by RSPCA inspectors serve the same purpose as those of the police and are required to be filled in accurately in detail on a daily basis. Likewise, they can be and often are produced in court during prosecutions concerning cruelty to animals.

The first thing that struck me as I accompanied Ted on his calls, apart from the thick smog emerging from his trusty briar, was the fact that there was no Securicor or other firm's radio in the vehicle. It transpired that, in those days, there was no national scheme to equip the inspectorate vans with radio communication that would enable emergency and other calls to be passed on promptly. An individual inspector might persuade his local branch to pay for a system to be fitted, but few branches were wealthy enough to oblige their inspector to that extent. Consequently, most inspectors took calls at home in the morning, at lunchtime and early in the evening. When they were out or otherwise unavailable an answering machine would relay a message telling callers to try again later or, in the case of an emergency, to ring the police or a veterinary surgeon for advice. Barely believable now, of course, but very much the way of things with the RSPCA back then. For many years the Society had to be dragged screaming and protesting into the prevailing times. In many instances it would be no exaggeration to say it was shamed into keeping up with beneficial new technology and operating procedures.

The only vaguely memorable event of my first day in Stafford with Ted was meeting Travelling Superintendent Hilton at his house in Lichfield. The ranks and structure of the Inspectorate are mystifying, but suffice to say TS Hilton was the big beast in the field round those parts. As such, he showed absolutely no interest in a microbe like me, not even examining and signing my notebook – something every other travelling superintendent I encountered insisted upon. To be honest, I hardly had time to form a lasting opinion of the chap as we were off again and hitting the road in no time.

'You know who he is, then?' asked Ted.

'The travelling superintendent?'

'Aye!' He could see I was struggling. 'His lad's in that famous pop group . . .'

My imagination ran riot. 'What . . . you don't mean T Rex?'

Ted gave me a look of despair. Clearly, I had aimed too high. It was his turn to struggle as he couldn't think of the group's name. I threw in what I thought were a few likely candidates.

'The Kinks . . . the Who . . . Status Quo. Maybe Genesis?'

'No . . . something to do with raincoats.' That floored me. I couldn't think of anything even remotely suitable.

It was as we were parking at Penkridge Horse Sale that Ted suddenly remembered the group's name.

'Fleetwood Mac! Aye, that's it!' Raincoats indeed.

There was a lot of market work in the Stafford area and a lot of markets that needed attending . . . Stafford itself, Stone, Eccleshall and, of course, the horse sales at Penkridge Smithfield. We were always on the lookout for animals brought to market in an unfit condition, ones that should never have been transported and exposed for sale. Vehicles were checked for faults and loading and unloading supervised. Some of the drovers were far too handy with their sticks and the chief would intervene when necessary. The use of electric prods to encourage cattle into and out of vehicles and pens was often excessive and we made a point of monitoring their use and stopping any abuse. Ted was a well-respected figure in the local auction markets and rarely had to resort to threats to prosecute or even administer cautions. In fact most of the farmers and market staff let him know if they saw something wrong.

We were supervising the arrival of twenty store cattle and eight bullocks at Stone's big cattle and sheep market one day when I noticed that the chief was paying particular attention to a lorry bringing in some cattle from up north.

'Him again,' he muttered.

'What's up, chief?'

'That bloke in the red transporter – I had words with him only a fortnight since.'

It had started to rain, a thick curtain of drizzle, as we walked over to the vehicle. It had obviously seen better days and was in a pretty dilapidated condition. The ramp used to load and unload livestock had only a few struts remaining to keep their feet from sliding underneath them, and one of the side gates preventing animals from falling off the ramp was missing. There were only a few wisps of damp straw bedding inside and some very dangerous edges and projections were visible which could have injured livestock during the journey.

'Hello?' The chief tapped on the driver's half-open door. A small wiry man dropped down to the ground looking apprehensive.

'Canna help?' he asked in a Geordie accent.

'Arthur, isn't it?'

'Aye, that's it.'

'All right, Arthur, you're not deaf nor daft that I know of. Just a couple of weeks ago we went through a list of things that are wrong with your wagon and I told you to fix them pronto. Am I right?' He paused for an answer. I didn't know it then but I was about to hear for the first time a phrase that would become a standing joke amongst inspectors up my way:

'Well . . . it's like this!'

'Like what?'

'The boss says he's replacin' this wi' a brand spankin' new one, as soon as. So what's the sense spendin' good money on this 'un?' I never saw Ted get really angry but he came close to it then.

'The only reason I'm allowing you to unload,' he barked, 'is because those animals are exhausted and there's every chance of an injury occurring inside the wagon. We'll get an old door out of storage to act as your missing side gate and scatter some more straw on the ramp.'

As the cattle were unloaded into nearby pens they were slipping and sliding in the wet conditions. They were clearly in poor bodily condition and urgently needed rest – together with food and water, which we made sure were provided. At the end of the lengthy operation the chief took Arthur to one side and cautioned him to the effect that 'the book' would be thrown at him if he ever appeared with the same wagon in the same state at any Staffordshire market again. Further questioning revealed that the cattle were off a farm up Lancaster way owned by the man who ran the transport business – Arthur's boss in fact. Ted made a note.

When things had settled down again we had a bit of a break in the old market cafe – a cuppa and a rather tasty raspberry bun. Ted could see I'd enjoyed our snack and went to get another bun, which he collected from the rather good-looking young woman behind the counter and dropped on my plate with a grin on his face.

'What's up, chief?'

'Oh, just that the young lady seems to have taken a shine to you, Steve. Asked your name she did.' I looked up and sure enough, there she was, eyeing me up between serving her other customers. It reminded me of Kathie back home and how much I missed her. Ted got his pipe out, and after he'd lit the thing to his, if nobody else's, satisfaction he turned to me, nodding his head knowingly. 'Oh, yes, I nearly forgot. She said she's glad you liked her buns!'

The next morning I walked round to the chief's place as usual from my digs at Weeping Cross to find the travelling superintendent already there. He must have set off early from Lichfield, so something big was brewing for sure. As before, my presence was ignored and he spoke in low, secretive tones to Ted while I made the tea. Then, just as I'd finished, he was off, leaving his tea to go cold. Strangely, I never discovered what the big secret was before my month in Stafford was up.

'What's with the super?' I enquired. Ted looked at me rather oddly. 'Tell you later. I've got a call to make.' He picked up the phone and I picked up the morning paper. Twenty minutes later he explained that he'd been on to the Lancaster and Morecambe inspector in north Lancashire, passing him the details of Arthur's boss and asking him to visit his place as soon as possible. Ted thought there might be serious cause for concern regarding the welfare of animals at the farm after the incident at Stone. Anyway, better to be on the safe side.

'Where are we off to today?' I asked as he struggled to light his overworked briar.

'I'm going shopping with the wife. It's my day off. I've arranged for you to spend the day with Inspector Wells from Birmingham. He should be here any minute.'

My day with the lad from Brum was probably my worst to date on the course – although Reading abattoir ran it pretty close. It started steadily enough with an alleged abandonment of a rough-coated terrier in Palmerston Road. As it turned out, the dog had actually been collected the previous evening by its owners. Then it was on to a local vet to discuss an outstanding invoice, and finally we landed at Barnes Hill Animal Centre where I met the area branch secretary. She was a mountainous woman with an unnervingly deep voice and acute halitosis. When I'd applied for the job something about a branch secretary had been mentioned and I'd imagined some sort of private secretary available to do all the necessary typing of reports, complaint forms and case files. But no – a secretary in reality was the head of whatever local branch an inspector might be sent to serve in England and Wales. In effect she was yet another boss. I rapidly discovered that a weekly appearance at the branch secretary's house or a meeting at the branch clinic or kennels was expected. In those days, if a branch didn't take to an inspector allocated to them by

headquarters he or she might well find themselves transferred whether they liked it or not. I soon realized that,
like any other inspector, I had to type all my paperwork
myself. In a busy area this meant doing it in your own
time, before or after duty periods or on days off. To get
behind with your office work was a cardinal sin, and those
who struggled in that regard didn't usually make it to a
long-service medal no matter how well suited they were to
the job otherwise.

Inspector Wells showed me round Barnes Hill, which
took some time. It was a big place and I was impressed with
the up-to-date facilities and the obvious commitment of the
staff to the animals in their care. Still, I was beginning to
wonder how much I was actually learning when he casually
opened the door to a small room down a corridor away
from the main building. As we entered he explained that this
was where the animals were 'put to sleep'. I looked round
and noted half a dozen metal chloroform chambers on the
bench, a stack of cat traps and cages over in the far corner,
a large freezer and, hanging behind the door, a great tangle
of old dog leads and collars, some still with their name discs
attached – 'My name is Paddy', 'Bess' and 'Scamper' – followed by a phone number. Now, Birmingham I know is a
very big place, the country's second city as it likes to call
itself, and the Barnes Hill centre acted as the stray kennels for a large area, but, even so, I couldn't believe what
followed. A row of dogs suddenly appeared in the corridor
outside, some on leads and others in the arms of kennel
staff. The queue seemed to grow by the minute.

'What's happening?' I said, my voice low.

'We'll be assisting with the euthanasia today,' announced Wells. 'It's listed here that you've not done this before . . . is that right?'

'Yes, that's . . . right!' I stuttered, knowing that I'd suddenly walked into my worst nightmare almost without realizing it. Wells went through the techniques again that I'd learned at headquarters – fill the needle and expel any air; shave the area on the dog's leg; squeeze the leg to pump up the vein; insert the needle; draw blood to check you're in position and inject the pentobarbitone. So easy when you're not there doing it, when there's no emotion in the equation. Then there's the constant fear of messing up and causing the animal discomfort and pain. I had to euthanase six of the long line of dogs but more kept on arriving all the time. When we'd finished the final total was twenty-six and I was weary both physically and mentally. We were surrounded by bulging black bags and kennel staff cleaning and mopping everywhere. I can honestly say it was the most mind-numbing and depressing experience I'd ever endured. Some of the dogs had been aged or sick but some had been strays it had proved impossible to home for one reason or another. I tried to avoid their eyes and concentrate on what I was doing, but sometimes I'd look up and experience an overpowering sense of guilt and betrayal.

'Did you arrange that especially for my benefit?' I asked Wells.

'No,' he replied. 'It's like this, to a greater or lesser

extent, every time. There are so many unwanteds as well as the old and sick ones. An eye-opener, isn't it?' I nodded. My used syringe was still in my hand and I dropped it into the nearby sink.

On our way back to Stafford I asked Wells his opinion.

'You'll do.'

There was silence for a while.

'I hated doing it.'

'Of course. If you ever feel any different bloody well resign!' I understood exactly what he meant.

The next day I was out with the chief and we stopped to deliver four large boxes of clothes, books and other bric-a-brac at the local branch secretary's. That evening it was the annual branch fair and, as usual, she was organizer in chief of the event. Everything had been donated by local supporters and there was a lot of it judging by the amount of stuff cluttering her hall and stairway. The branch was set to make a healthy profit from the looks of things. Mind you, they needed to. Every year they had to send headquarters a good few thousand quid for the upkeep of their inspector; then there was the local clinic or a voucher scheme to run to assist the less well off and see that their animals got prompt treatment in case of illness and injury. Some branches also ran kennels or shelters, and raising enough to cover all their costs was a real headache for the volunteers involved at local level. Ted helped out whenever possible and attended all the fairs, fetes, open days and monthly branch meetings if other duties and emergencies allowed. He used to say, 'Keep 'em sweet and they'll see you all right!' It was good advice, as I was to find out later. At the monthly meetings the local inspector reports his figures for the month – complaints, cautions and market and circus visits. He also details the number of animals he's rehomed or had to euthanase before telling the tales of any outstanding rescues carried out. After a short question and answer period the inspector usually leaves and the committee is free to discuss the other items on the agenda.

Ted and I were recruited to help on one of the stalls at the fair that evening. We had to shake a few hands and make ourselves generally useful, which we proceeded to do. It was also expected that we'd buy something for ourselves, which presented a challenge on a probationer's wages. I scoured the various stalls, sometimes examining expensive items and bringing anticipatory smiles to several old ladies' faces before edging along to the next table, shamefaced.

'Bought anything?' It was the chief. He had a couple of books under one arm and a mince pie in his free hand.

'Still looking, I'm afraid.'

'Well, just grab something. I want to be off soon or we'll get lumbered putting stuff back into boxes. I don't mind helping out but there's a limit after a hard day's graft.' He took a look at the stall himself. 'What about that?'

'That' was a ceramic owl about five inches high and, to my mind, completely naff. Distinctly unimpressed at first, I suddenly remembered that the Oldham Athletic club badge featured an owl, and hesitated. 'How much is it?'

'Ninety-nine pence,' said Ted. 'But I know Jean on the stall here, don't I? Wait a minute.'

Walking round the back of the table, Ted had a few words with the blue-rinsed Jean, who was wearing a yellow 'royal family' pinny and Edna Everage specs.

'You can have it for fifty pence, seein' as it's you and she's a soft spot for probationers.'

There was no way I was going to be a cheapskate and as soon as Ted's back was turned I gave a pound for the owl and waited while Jean wrapped it in newspaper and nestled it in an old shoebox. Proudly I carried my prize away, certain that it would grace our mantelpiece for many years. Surely Kathie would approve?

November fifth that year was a Monday. I had leave to go home for the weekend of the third and fourth and took a train back to Manchester on the Friday evening. Mum had baked one of her majestic apple pies, which she'd learned how to make from my grandmother. The pastry was out of this world, so soft and smooth it actually melted in the mouth. No one has ever made pastry to match it in my experience – and I like my apple pies. Gran had been cook and housekeeper to no less a personage than Sir Geoffrey Fitzhervey de Montmorency, Governor of the Punjab, on his return to England. He settled in Cambridge and she was with him till he died, so she must have been a fair cook and all. Mum had obviously inherited some of Gran's skills along with her recipies.

Our small bonfire that Saturday evening on the unmade track behind our house was a pale imitation of the fires I'd enjoyed in my younger days. Three or four of us lads would collect anything that would burn from late September onwards: bits of old fencing, wood from derelict buildings, timber from broken-down garages and even old tyres. We stored it in yards and gardens, and on the day of the fire we'd drag it up in skips to Berries Field, so nobody got the chance to snaffle our stuff. Those big basketwork skips with their wooden runners were much prized and you could only get them from sympathetic friends or relatives who worked in one of the many cotton mills in our neighbourhood. Nearby were the Hawthorn, the Manor and the Busk, but mainly we got ours via close neighbours John Cooper and Dick Skelton who both worked at the Kent mill on Victoria Street.

Health and safety hadn't been invented then. Lads would set off bangers inside upturned skips folk were sitting on and aim rockets dead straight up in the air in the hope they'd frighten someone to death by landing near them. At least we had the sense to let an adult, usually my mate Ian Raynor's dad, light the bonfire. During the evening the mums would start to arrive with black peas, hot pot and delicious home-made parkin. Later, when the flames had died down, we'd stick potatoes and chestnuts into the hot embers where they cooked beautifully. The chestnuts popped and exploded when they were done and guaranteed a belly-ache later for the greedy or unwary.

Still, much the best thing about our little bonfire in 1973 was the time I got to spend with Kathie. Mum and Dad were quickly indoors after the fireworks and we had the rest of the evening to ourselves. Sitting close together on a couple of old chairs with our blue and white Latics bobble hats and scarves on we looked like two lovelorn pixies gazing into the dying flames and an uncertain future. Suddenly, a hot chestnut popped from the fire and landed in my lap. In my panic to brush it off, I fell off my chair and ended up in a heap in the long grass. We laughed about it long into the night.

# FIVE

My second period of field training was soon at hand. After a short break back home when I had what was left of my hair cut and reshaped and, with Kathie, witnessed the mighty top-of-the-table Latics thrash the Cherries of Bournemouth 4–2 in a terrific match at Boundary Park, it was time to catch the 7.18 train from Manchester to Peterborough. It had turned into a murky, drab, brass monkeys of a Monday morning and my battered old suitcase seemed heavier than ever as I lugged it on board the train. Unable to see much due to a thick mist hanging over the suburbs and the countryside, I glanced down at my ticket, number 1445, which had cost me just two pounds and eighty-five pence – about the price of a modest bus ride nowadays.

On arriving at Peterborough station I grabbed some lunch and waited outside on the station steps for Chief Inspector Mike Goodenough to arrive. Dead on time, a van emblazoned with the RSPCA logo pulled in close by. The passenger door flew open and I had my first glimpse of my new chief. A tall man, well over six feet, his huge frame was crammed uncomfortably into the driver's seat. He had a craggy face and his eyes bored into me with a sort of 'welcome to the real world' expression. Mike sported a neat crew cut on top, and when I looked down his big boots were so shiny I could have used them as a mirror for shaving. A relative shorthouse with a big suitcase must have been a terrible disappointment but he never let on.

'Hop in,' he yelled. I landed my suitcase on top of a pair of cat baskets parked between the seats and a dog guard and we set off for the digs he'd arranged for me in Park Road.

'How did you recognise me, chief?'

'There weren't too many candidates. It was between you with your suitcase and a middle-aged mum with a Mothercare catalogue carrying shopping bags. By the way, it's Mike. No standing on ceremony between ourselves. Steve, isn't it?' I nodded, both pleased and a little surprised. We cruised along Park Road, Mike looking along the lines of houses with odd numbers before pulling up at the one he wanted. Unlike the smart modern bungalow at the end of a cul-de-sac I'd stayed in while training at Stafford, the large terraced property looked a bit poky and run down from the outside. It looked much the same on the inside, I soon discovered. I was booked in and we left my case in my room on the second floor. First impressions can be notoriously misleading but on this occasion they were spot on. The place was definitely what you'd call basic. There were a few sticks of furniture, including a bed whose tired springs had clearly sprung in more than a few places already. The door of the utility wardrobe was half hanging off and there were no coat hangers inside. The old, grubby wallpaper was stained greyish-yellow with cigarette smoke. A tattered curtain hung at the one small window and a dust-coated Gideon Bible lay ignored on the shaky bedside table. Welcome to Peterborough. The local football team might be called 'the Posh' but as for my digs . . . blimey!

Back on the road we headed out to Somersham to investigate a complaint concerning a bay mare. Being a towny I'd not had a lot to do with horses. Although we'd had lectures on 'The Points of a Horse' and various related topics I hardly felt knowledgeable on the subject at that stage so it was a job I was looking forward to tackling – with Mike at hand, of course. We touched upon Farcet Fen and ran on through Pondersbridge and Ramsey, eventually arriving in Somersham around mid-afternoon. That in itself was fine but, like many complaints inspectors receive, this one lacked exact details of the location. We drove round Somersham and district in circles for twenty minutes or more. Mike was the lucky possessor of a Securicor radio in his vehicle, provided at the expense of the local branch and he called in to get more info.

'Delta King 132 to base.'

'Can I help you?' came the reply, together with a good deal of coughing and spluttering from the young lass on duty.

'Are you all right?'

'Sorry . . . tea break . . . chocolate biscuit. You caught

me in mid-munch.' Mike shook his head and we both burst out laughing.

'As long as you're all right, can you phone a Mrs Knighton at Warboys? You've got her number. Get the exact details of the animal's location, will you? And I do mean exact.'

'Roger. I'll get back to you soonest.'

It turned out that the mare was now in a field just off the B1050, nearer to a place called Colne than Somersham. Little did I know then that I'd soon be getting jobs myself in a very different town of the same name in my own area. We arrived at the right location – only to find an empty field.

'What do we do now, Mike?'

'Find any doors hereabouts and knock on them,' he advised. An old dear in a cottage up the road told us the horse belonged to a young couple who were splitting up.

'She lives in Fenton, he's from Wood End or Bluntisham, and they take turns havin' the mare nearer to one or the other. Poor thing don't know if it's coming or going bein' moved around so.'

'It'll be on its way back to the wife now?' ventured Mike.

'Surely. She came for it not half an hour ago. She's a ten-acre field off Church Road in Somersham.'

'We probably passed each other on our way here. Ridiculous really,' said Mike. 'There's not four or five miles the difference.'

We finally caught up with the elusive animal in Somersham and encouraged her over to the gate of the field where we could examine her more thoroughly. She looked terribly thin to me and I suspected a possible case of cruelty.

'Should I get on the radio, Mike?'

'What for?'

'To get a vet out to see the horse . . . she's really, really thin, isn't she?'

Mike smiled. 'No need, Steve. Look at her; sway backed, high hipped. The feet are all right. And look in the field. There's an old bathtub full of water over there and plenty of signs of supplementary feeding.'

I looked and learned. 'I see what you mean.'

'There's a shed for shelter by the fence over there. As we'll both find out, and me a lot sooner than you, there's no cure for old age. I just hope there's someone looking out for me same as this old girl. Still, I'll leave a card on the gate and have a word about shifting her around. Stupid that is. I'll suggest a vet check her regularly too but I'll bet that's being done already.'

As Somersham wasn't near any of Mike's other calls he drove straight back to Peterborough and dropped me off at my digs late in the afternoon. Absence, in this case, had not made the heart grow fonder – Alaska House still looked poky, grubby and in need of a good lick of paint.

Once inside, I met plump Mrs Blake who ran the place with Ernie her armchair husband. In the four weeks I was there I don't recall ever seeing him upright, never mind doing a spot of work. Mrs Blake told me not to put too much weight on the banister as it 'moved about a bit'. She

also made a point of emphasizing the strict meal times –
dinner was 6 to 7.30 p.m., breakfast 6.30 to 7.30 a.m. It
was a case of turn up on time or don't turn up at all.

I soon found out that I was far from the only paying guest
at Mrs Blake's. There were at least six others, all Irish lads
working on the roads, real-life Boys from the Blackstuff. I
got to know one of them, name of Patrick, pretty well. We
were about the same age and into similar music. He was
forever inviting me down to the local pub where he was the
fiddle player in an Irish folk band. One evening I decided to
take him up on the offer. Blimey, could those lads sup ale.
Well, Guinness and chasers in the main which, together
with the excellent music, generated a great atmosphere
and a very thick head the next day. I'm lucky really in that
if I drink too much I'm usually ill before I can do too much
damage to myself. I was certainly ill back at our digs that
night. Patrick knocked on my door the following morning
as I hadn't gone down for breakfast as usual.

'Come in,' I mumbled, my head banging and feeling like
a lead weight on my shoulders. I propped myself up on
my pillows as he entered looking as bright and breezy as a
spring morning.

'You've missed your breakfast, Stevie boy. What's the
matter?'

'Hey, quiet, Pat . . . my head!'

He laughed. 'You know what'll cure you, don't you?'

'No. But you're going to tell me, aren't you?'

'Another pint of Black . . . hair of the dog and all that.'

I threw one of the pillows at him and missed. 'What's

the time?' I asked, rubbing my eyes and shaking my muzzy head.

'Well . . . let's see now. The big hand's past eight and the little hand's nearly touching nine.'

'Oh . . . right!' The implications didn't immediately register with me. Then, suddenly, they did. Quarter to nine and I was supposed to be at the chief's house on the hour. I shot out of my creaking bed, washed and dressed in a flash and caught the bus in record time. Even so, it was gone half past nine when I knocked on Mike's door, wondering what the response would be. He was on the phone and shouted for me to come in. Inside the hallway I bumped into his wife Margo on her way out.

'Hello,' she said. 'You look a bit worse for wear.'

'I was out on the town last night. Overslept this morning. I'd probably still be in bed if one of the lads at my digs hadn't rousted me out. Mike's not going to be happy, is he?'

'Don't worry. He's in a good mood. You look frozen. Come through to the kitchen and I'll make a cup of coffee for you.'

'You'll be late for work . . . like me!'

'Never mind. Come on.' That was Margo for you – one smashing lady. I wish I could have spent more time getting to know her. She was great to talk to and made you feel at ease.

As soon as Mike finished his call and saw that Margo had taken me under her wing he just laughed and told me not to be late again. When Margo left, he picked up his boots and began spit-polishing them.

'All you need in the morning, Steve . . . a shit, a shave and a shoeshine. After that you're ready to take on the world.' Later, I added a shower to Mike's list and found it was excellent advice.

Before we set off the phone rang and Mike answered. I put on my uniform coat and gloves before venturing out into the chill autumn air to unlock the van. A few minutes later Mike joined me.

'Swop!' he said, indicating I should occupy the driver's seat.

'What?'

'You're driving. Here.' He threw me the keys. It came as a pleasant surprise to be allowed to drive the firm's vehicle – something Ted in Stafford had never let me do.

'You sure, Mike?'

'You've got a licence, haven't you?'

'Yes.'

'You drive home most weekends from Horsham, I'm told.'

'We hire a car between four of us and take turns to drive and keep it over the two days.'

'Well, the point is you're obviously a good driver. And if you weren't you'd need the practice anyway. You'll be driving a lot while you're here.'

'Where to?

'We'll do that last call in Silver Street first . . . Mrs Humphries. Her old dog's fifteen and very arthritic. She can't afford the vet so she rang us.'

'There's no clinic or welfare centre, then?'

'No.'

We arrived in Silver Street and were met at her front door by Mrs Humphries, who was seventy-six years old and just about the thinnest human being I have ever set eyes upon to this day. She assured us several times that she wasn't ill, but she clearly wasn't eating anything like enough.

'Have you got much in the fridge, dear?' Mike asked, and went over and opened it. The compartments were all reasonably well stocked but almost entirely with food for her dog. Looking round, the house was spotlessly clean and tidy but there was no sign of the animal.

'Did you do as I asked?' said Mike.

'Yes. It's his favourite spot at the bottom of the garden where he liked to wander.'

'Where is he?'

'Upstairs . . . I'll go and get him.' A few minutes later she came tottering down, almost falling, with her dog painfully struggling on a lead behind her.

'What's his name then?' I enquired.

'Jasper.'

Mike and I quickly made friends with the little black and white crossbreed then left his owner alone with him to say goodbye. Outside in the back garden Mike checked the mechanism of his .32 Webley Scott humane killer.

'You don't use the injection method, Mike?'

'Nah. Ex-army, you see. I reckon it's the fastest and kindest way – best for the animal.'

Mrs Humphries joined us and stoically handed Jasper over to the chief and we walked him to the grave that had been dug at the bottom of the garden. Mrs Humphries wanted him buried there and, on Mike's instructions, she'd had her grandson dig the grave in a favourite spot between a clump of ancient rhubarb and a sprawling magnolia bush. As we led him slowly along the little dog's hindquarters swayed stiffly from side to side and he threatened to collapse on a couple of occasions. We stopped by the side of the grave and Mike prepared his gun before gently placing the tip to the head of the dog. He told me to stand well back but I hesitated and, suddenly, it was all over. There was the boom of the gunshot, which left me partially deaf for three days, and the instant collapse of the animal with no time for suffering in between. As Mike said, a bullet travelling at six hundred miles an hour over a distance of just three or four inches is as humane a demise as you can get. Of course, there's more to it than that. Steady nerves and the ability to put the animal at ease only come with experience. Not everyone is cut out to use this method which, in any case, has lost favour nowadays, not being exactly politically correct. It has to be done outdoors, there's always blood, however small the amount, it's only applicable to dogs and large animals and there's a chance, however unlikely, of something going horrendously wrong; all these things have contributed to its ultimate abandonment. Nevertheless, having witnessed the procedure at first hand I was fairly impressed back then and couldn't argue with Mike's point that any period of suffering was reduced to virtually zero. For the first couple of years after my appointment as a fully fledged inspector I adopted Mike's method whenever possible and followed his quiet, careful approach when faced with one of the worst aspects of the job.

We found Mrs Humphries slumped in an armchair in the living room. Her watery eyes shone bravely as she tried to keep the tears behind them in check. Seeing her, I quickly found myself doing the same. Mike, though he had experienced this situation many times before and had a full list of jobs that day, still took time to comfort her.

'Have you anyone to come in and sit with you for a while?'

'It's all right,' she said. 'My grandson, Luke, will be along later. He's a good lad, you know. We'll bury Jasper together. I'll be fine.'

Life's not fair, we all know – though some better than others – but it's also weird and incomprehensible. A small black and white crossbred dog, the type that might be cruelly and thoughtlessly abandoned at the chance of a holiday by some owners, can be cared for by others as part of the family, or an elderly person's best friend and companion. It's just chance, I suppose, but it never ceases to amaze me. I first heard the words 'When you're born you need a lucky ticket to last you a lifetime' on a TV show . . . Dennis Waterman was the actor, I think. I reckon there's a lot in that, and old Jasper certainly got one in so far as his owner loved and cared for him and saw to it that he didn't suffer at the end of a good and long life.

'How long will it be before Luke gets here?' said Mike.

'A couple of hours.'

'Right. Steve here will stay and have a cup of Rosie Lee with you and I'll do a few jobs in the neighbourhood. How's that?' Before Mrs Humphries could argue Mike was pointing me in the direction of the kitchen and the kettle, saying goodbye and letting himself out. He was gone about an hour and a half and I managed to get Mrs H talking about her life as a nurse in Cambridge, which started me on about my gran and Sir Geoffrey. Of course, Jasper dominated the conversation and his photograph album ended up on the table. Strangely, there were no tears. Talking to me about him seemed to provide some comfort.

Later, back on the road with Mike, I asked him where he'd been. Apparently, the two calls he'd made were NRs, no replies, so he'd spent the time stripping down, oiling and cleaning his Webley Scott, which he emphasized was necessary every time it was used. It made me wonder if my time might have been better spent watching him cleaning the gun. He must have read my thoughts.'You were learning something back there, you know. I can show you the other stuff any time and I will, but not what you learned at Mrs H's.'

'What was that, then?'

'Compassion. Sometimes, especially if you're run off your feet, it doesn't get a look in and there's not even time for a moment or two to reflect.'

'But they tell us at headquarters not to get emotionally involved or we'll not be able to do the job at all.'

'I'm not saying you should get emotionally involved,'

said Mike, 'but respect the feelings of those who are and make an effort to acknowledge them.'

It was probably at that moment that I began to fully comprehend why trainees were sent to people such as Mike and, to a lesser extent, Ted in Stafford. It was essential, especially for younger trainees such as myself, and would be invaluable later when we were left to run our own areas. Words and work in classrooms have their place, of course, but it would be our training in the field that we'd look to for guidance and inspiration when faced with problems of our own. Naturally, as an inspector, you could always phone headquarters for advice, but I know that whenever I resorted to it I always felt a bit of a wally and a failure. The only downside of being with Mike was wondering if I could ever do the job remotely as well. I remember I was with him at Stamford market when a young drover the size of a brick proverbial started moving some cattle. His method involved the liberal and well-out-of-order use of a stick. Despite the fact that this lad was even an inch or two taller than he was, Mike went over to 'have words' with him. Two minutes later the big lad was behaving himself and gave no hint of trouble afterwards. I tackled Mike in the van on our way back to his house. 'There's no way I could have got a result like that with that drover.'

'Why not? What matters is how you come over to people. If they think you're being fair and talking sense they'll clock the uniform and take notice, believe me.' Of course, he was right again. It wasn't just what he taught you that made Mike the perfect mentor but the confidence he instilled too. You can't turn base metal into gold, but I'd be amazed if any trainee who was lucky enough to be assigned to Peterborough went on to fail the course.

That evening, during another spectacularly bad meal at my digs, something started to itch at the back of my left shoulder. Just annoying at first, it developed into a major embarrassment and nothing I did relieved the discomfort for more than a moment or two. Back in my room with the use of a mirror I found there was a small white patch in the area that was giving me gip. I thought I'd been nettled or something, which made no sense at all as the area had been covered all day. Luckily, Patrick called with another drinking invite, took one look and solved the mystery. 'It's a bite you've got – a pig flea. I've had one or two meself lodgin' here and there.'

'A pig flea!' My thoughts returned to the market at Stamford that afternoon; I had handled some pigs in one of the pens. Clearly, an unwelcome guest had travelled back with me. 'Is it still there?' I asked him.

'Oh, it'll be there all right – under yer skin. That little dot is the opening it breathes through. Put some Vaseline over it, if you like, or I'll get him out for you with the old hot needle.' The Vaseline method was preferable, I thought, as the idea of someone who wasn't a nurse or a doctor sticking a hot needle under my skin didn't exactly appeal. Then it started to really itch again and I thought of the flea gorging itself, making a meal of my blood.

'Have you got one – a needle?'

He nodded and fetched one from his room. We sterilized it with boiling water from the kettle and Patrick went to work.

'There!' he announced triumphantly. 'Got the booger!' Suddenly, the spot of pain seemed worth it. TCP and a plaster completed the job. I thanked Patrick and told him he should definitely give up the blackstuff and take up doctoring but I didn't join him at the pub. I'd learned my lesson after the last time. Besides, my too-close encounter with *Pulex irritans*, the pig or human flea, had tired me out. I had been going to write a letter home and another to Kathie but I decided to leave them over to the next day. I wondered just how much of my blood the little blighter had filched – it felt like an armful. Sleep, on an empty arm and a largely empty stomach, came to me quickly that night.

Funny how things happen unexpectedly. It started off just an ordinary day like any other. Mike had arranged to pick me up from my digs that morning and after a quick call at the vet's we made our way to Stonebridge Farm at Thorney where an aggressive stray dog was proving quite impossible to catch. In those days, of course, there were no dog wardens employed by the local authority to deal with such situations and it fell to RSPCA inspectors to find a solution. The owner of the farm had tried to feed the animal into a barn and shut the door on it, without success. As it was a bitch in pup it needed to be caught sooner rather than later or things could get complicated. A large dog trap seemed the best bet but Peterborough branch didn't have one. Mike promised to get hold of the Cambridge inspector in order to borrow their brand new one and bring it along to the farm as soon as possible. Murphy's law dictated that the dog wasn't around at the time of our visit so we had to leave it at that.

As we headed off to tackle the next few calls on Mike's list I started to take in the incredible fenland landscape we were driving through. I've visited most of Britain on holidays, weekends away and day trips over the years but it was an area that was completely new to me then, with a feel and an atmosphere all its own. The vast flatlands' horizon seemed endless, only interrupted by the occasional farmbuilding or isolated willow or poplar tree. The whole area had been reclaimed from the sea and, somehow, it gave me the impression that one day the sea would be back, fierce and irresistible, to claim its own. The road we were on undulated at regular intervals and the dips, though mainly shallow, left me queasy.

Accompanying us were dark and empty crop fields that seemed to stretch for ever into the distance, and by the roadside were broad ditches and dykes with rough grass growing up their sides, full of freezing cold water. The utter solitude and the bleak emptiness of the unchanging landscape was profound, and late on a winter's afternoon when mist begins to form it can seem eerie and threatening. I'm one who appreciates time to myself, preferably where there's no reception for a mobile phone and a pub's within walking distance. Fenland's quiet all right, with a weird beauty all of its own, but I couldn't help feeling slightly uneasy driving through the area. I was reminded of Sherlock Holmes' remarks on the countryside: 'its isolation and the impunity with which crime may be committed there. The lowest and vilest alleys in London do not present a more dreadful record of sin than does the smiling and beautiful countryside.'

We finally found ourselves back in Thorney having received an urgent call to nearby Newborough. 'If the complaint's justified this could be a case,' Mike told me. 'Make sure everything goes down in your notebook. Here we are . . . Northborough Road.' We pulled up next to a smallholding about the size of a large pen up north. Back at the training school in Horsham there'd been a lot of speculation about who'd 'get lucky' and hit upon a case of cruelty during field training. There's no substitute for hands-on experience and it looked as though I might be amongst the fortunate few.

We clambered over some ramshackle fencing and walked over to a huge stack of straw in the middle of the smallholding. Nearby, a metal stake had been driven into the ground and an Alsatian bitch on just three feet of chain was barking a greeting to us. She had two well-fed six-week-old pups running around her. Given that she was still feeding the pups her bodily condition was good. Surprisingly, it didn't take long to gain her confidence and handling her was no problem. She was far from the usual guard dog often met with on pens and smallholdings and it went against the grain to find a dog with her nature and temperament in that situation. The chief made a close examination of the mother while I kept the pups away and made a fuss of them.

'Come and look at this,' said Mike. I went over to look with a sense of foreboding. There was something in the tone of his voice that suggested 'this' would be deeply unpleasant. At the end of the short chain the dog had a collar of plastic binder twine wrapped twice round its neck, which had obviously been in place for some time. It had cut some three quarters of an inch into the neck muscles, causing a pus-ridden, suppurating wound that circled the throat and right round the back of the neck. In places the twine was invisible, buried under scab and dead tissue an inch wide.

'Hell, Mike. How could this . . .' My voice tailed off and, for a moment, I couldn't speak.

'Twine's been used instead of a suitable collar when the dog was a lot younger and never checked or adjusted since. Best get a vet out to see this and remove the twine. He may have to knock her out to shift it all, as the wound's so wide and deep. I've never seen anything quite like it. What sort of blighted mentality would allow it to happen? I'll never understand people responsible for things like this.'

Later, when I'd been in the job a few years and accumulated a fair number of cases of my own, I understood how Mike felt that day in the fens. When you're faced with the outer limits of human stupidity and cruelty, mixed with the natural disgust and revulsion is a yearning to understand. Yet the people involved rarely offer a rational explanation for the suffering they've caused. During their interviews under caution, all sorts of half-cocked, illogical stuff comes out of their mouths that doesn't make sense at all. However, I began to realize after a time that, in some cases at least, it did to them. Which is pretty frightening really.

Mike went back to the van and got on the radio. He arranged for a vet to attend and then called his brother, who was a professional photographer. We waited with the dog and made sure she didn't pull on the chain and cause herself more pain and distress. John Goodenough arrived first and, after a brief confab with Mike, took the necessary pictures as evidence should court proceedings follow. Since they were brothers, there would be no charge to the Society for his services.

Leaving John with the dog, Mike and I began to explore.

'Have you noticed, Steve?' I hadn't. 'There's a hole in that stack of straw to act as a kennel for the bitch and her pups. Two pups are in there now. It's pretty snug and warm.'

I looked. 'Quite a good idea if only the bitch could get in it.'

'Exactly. Her chain's way too short.' Mike shook his head. 'It's crazy.'

It was clear to us that the owner of the animals must have a strange or sadistic personality. Here is someone who uses a pet dog to guard a smallholding, comes up regularly to feed the animals according to our information, and yet fails to notice or just ignores a twine collar gradually garrotting his dog. He builds a straw-stack shelter for the bitch and her pups and then makes it impossible for the mother to reach it. Surely, I thought, this was the stuff of straitjackets and sectioning under the Mental Health Act. Our further explorations uncovered a series of open, brick-built pens containing eight lame pigs with no bedding. Bodily, the animals were in decent condition but there was no food present and the water sinks were frozen over.

When the vet arrived a little later he managed to slowly and gently remove all the twine from the dog's neck without putting her under, mainly due to her superb temperament. She yelped a few times all right, but never offered to bite. More photographs were taken of her neck and the vet treated the wound and the surrounding area. He was just about finished when it started to snow. Big feathery flakes floated down out of the blanket of grey sky, gradually whitening paths, fields and roads and somehow adding to the surreal quality of the day. After discussing the situation with the vet I helped Mike replace the twine round the dog's neck with a soft, wide leather collar as a temporary measure. Then, with the snow turning to a thin drizzle, everyone departed and we were left alone to fill in our notebooks and wait for the owner of the animals to arrive.

As our breath steamed up the van's windows I began to think seriously about what had happened, how truly shocking it was and whether I'd be able to deal with similar situations on my own. Anyone faced with cruelty, to animals or humans, naturally gets angry and outraged and so they should. But as RSPCA inspectors we were charged with doing something positive about it, collecting evidence and following legal procedures to the letter lest a prosecution fail because of some simple mistake on an inspector's part, all the while staying calm, collected and focused. It meant putting aside, virtually shutting out, the basic emotional response. I had watched Mike closely and at every step he'd remained firmly in control of the situation and his emotions. Anticipating court proceedings, he'd brought in the vet and the photographer. It had not been a difficult decision on this occasion, but there are many instances, as I was to discover later, where such judgements are far from clear cut. Getting it wrong meant wasting the Society's and its supporters' money or, on the other hand, possibly leaving an animal suffering or in danger of doing so. The responsibility that came with the job was huge, almost overwhelming. What we were really dealing with was the unthinkable, the unthinkable that had actually happened. Few people who knew me back then, friends or casual acquaintances, would have thought I could handle it. I decided right there and then in Mike's van, as we waited and talked with the heater on full blast, that I was going to prove them wrong. This was a job, career, call it what you like, where you could make a contribution that mattered, a real difference. It was the job for me.

About quarter to five in the afternoon he arrived. A neat, small man with receding dark hair. Nothing special about him that I could see. I was reminded of Leonard Cohen's poem about Eichmann. His appearance was quite ordinary – no green saliva, talons or madness.

He was an ex-patriot Polish ex-serviceman who had a

job at Perkins Engines in Peterborough. The smallholding was a sideline he visited once a day in the early evening and during the day at weekends. He claimed he didn't know about the dog's wound, which Mike insisted be further treated by the man's own vet that evening. We told him the bitch and pups should be given shelter, food, bedding and water inside a suitable enclosed area. That way she wouldn't have to be chained up and the wound would have the chance to heal. Advice regarding the pigs followed and Mike completed all the legal requirements before we left.

We returned to Newborough the next day. The pigs had straw, food and running water. A corrugated-iron shelter inside a pen had been constructed for the bitch and her pups and food and water provided. Plenty of straw bedding was around. Clearly, things were improving.

A prosecution for causing the dog unnecessary suffering followed and substantial fines and costs were awarded against the man responsible. Disappointingly, he was not banned by the court from keeping animals, a fact which, like Mike, I found difficult to accept. As he said later, 'There's the law all right, but there's not always justice.'

Just before my time in Peterborough was up we received a call that a swan had got a fish hook and line dangling from its beak on the river Nene.

'Fancy having a go at catching her?' asked Mike.

'I've never used a swan hook before but I'll have a go. Does the branch have a boat?'

He grinned. 'The branch don't but I do. Bought her recently. She's in good shape, too.'

'You never mentioned you had a boat, Mike.'

'I didn't have to. I knew we'd get a job on the river during your time here, although it's turned out to be a pretty close thing. I'm usually down there once a fortnight at least.'

When we arrived on the river after lunch that day it was cold and bright but the wind was getting up and causing a stir on the water. Mike began by showing me round his neat little Dolphin cruiser and pointed to a rubber dinghy with an outboard motor which we were going to use on the rescue. Faster and more manoeuvrable than the cruiser, it shouldn't alarm the swan if we approached with care and drifted in after cutting the engine. Remarkably, we caught the pen on my second attempt with the swan hook and I managed to get my arm round her powerful wings as we landed her in the boat. I was fully aware that a blow from one of them could break an arm. Once aboard, I kept her head down low with my free hand while Mike examined her. After a struggle he managed to get the whole lot out – line, float and hook – but there was visible damage and we decided to take her to a vet. I'm pleased to say that the swan recovered fully and a few days later we released her back on the river. Watching her sail away exercising her wings and clearly enjoying her freedom was tremendously satisfying and gave me a feeling of well-being a day in the office never could. I always felt the same when rescues ended in the recovery and release of a casualty.

A few days before Christmas Mike was due to deliver me to the railway station when, unexpectedly, the spare van in the region became available. I was allowed to keep it over the holiday period and drive down to Horsham with it at New Year. The vehicles were leased by the Society and this one was due for replacement, it seemed. I said goodbye to Mike and the wonderful Margo, thanking them for everything. It was a parting of firm friends.

On the long drive home I found myself wondering if I'd pass the training exams and get posted somewhere near Peterborough. At the time I wouldn't have minded any-where really, though it was difficult not to favour a move back north. Walsall, which I knew was a vacant station, would have been fine. Then again I'd spent happy holidays in Bude and Padstow so Cornwall beckoned. After a while I gave up thinking about it. The fact is your posting is a lottery and Kathie and I would have to make the best of it wherever we ended up.

Of course, I kept in touch with Mike and Margo via Christmas cards and messages, but it would be thirty-three years before I would meet them again.

# SIX

I didn't go down on one knee or smother her with red roses. I couldn't afford to hire a plane to fly over trailing an *I love you, Kathie Hanley* message in the sky. We weren't even at an expensive restaurant . . . only a seventies bistro in Union Street, Oldham. It was just after Christmas 1973 and I was determined to ask Kathie to marry me – again. We'd been going out together for a little over two and a half years when, about eighteen months ago, I'd first popped the question. She'd turned me down, believing it wasn't the right time. Our savings were accumulating more slowly than we'd like so I could see the problem in that respect. But this time things were very different and I hoped for a better result. Besides, she was getting prettier while I was just getting . . . older.

Our finances eighteen months on were much improved thanks to curbing expenses and the break-up of the band that I played in. Variously named MPL, Wandervögel and the dull and stupid Index we'd played all sorts of venues including folk clubs that we'd weaselled our way into some-how or other. Audiences expecting sea shanties and other traditional fare must have been stunned when we hit them with our own songs like 'Arbitrating Reflective Memorials' (don't ask) or the incredibly embarrassing 'You Made Me Feel Like a Man,' which had the sort of dodgy lyrics that make me squirm even now when I think of them. We sent some stuff off to the already legendary John Peel who, bril-liantly and unexpectedly, wrote back saying he personally had enjoyed it but thought his listeners might not be ready for it yet. Naturally, we took this as a compliment and pat-ted ourselves on the back for our originality. Very fine man was John, and much missed by all and sundry.

Regardless of the state of our finances, there was another factor in the equation which was brought home to me forcibly by the training superintendent, Len Flint, when the subject had come up. Married trainee inspectors would be allocated permanent stations while single officers could expect to be sent here, there and everywhere on temporary duty postings, despatched wherever a current manpower shortage was causing problems. It was obvious that Kathie and I would have to marry soon or be apart for long periods, which didn't bear thinking about. Fortunately, Kathie consented to be my wife and the ceremony was scheduled for 26 January at her local church. We'd have to forgo a honeymoon as such as I had to take final exams at headquarters starting on the 28th. Ridiculous really – let's face it, who in their right mind would get married in January if they could help it? – but we wanted to be together and being allocated a permanent station, wherever it might be, was the only way that was going to happen. When I told him I would be a married man before the course ended Len sent me an acknowledgement expressing his 'commiserations'.

On Sunday 30 December I kissed Kathie goodbye and drove down to Horsham and my digs, leaving her to make all the arrangements for the wedding. For myself, the first thing I had to do was get us somewhere to live. Staying with Marvin in the railwayman's cottage was out of the question, but enquiries in Horsham and the surrounding area soon made me realize that finding anywhere else wouldn't be easy. Like everything else in those parts, accommodation cost an arm and a leg, with a month in advance expected. There was no option but to look southwards to Brighton and the coast, where prices were generally lower. Within a week I'd secured a large room at a hotel on Norfolk Terrace in Brighton. It even had a sea view – if you stuck your head out of the window as far as possible and managed to look to the right without getting a crick in the neck. I paid the usual month in advance plus a returnable deposit before ringing Kathie with the good news. She didn't seem relieved or particularly pleased, her head achingly full of dress alterations and flower, photographer and reception arrangements. She asked if I was coming home that weekend and almost dissolved into tears when I told her I was on duty at Club Row animal market in London with no chance of a reprieve.

The big day finally arrived, and I wangled permission off the vicar to set up my old reel-to-reel tape recorder in the church near the lectern. We still have the recording, which was surprisingly good, and I recently copied it on to a CD.

Kathie and I spent our wedding night in a four-poster bed at a hotel in Stratford-upon-Avon. She was totally exhausted and I had a stinking cold. The next day we travelled down to Brighton and moved into our arranged accommodation. It was a large room on the top floor with a small kitchen area, a bath and a toilet. That night, I realized that we were sharing our room with at least one non-paying guest. Odd, annoying, scrabbling and scampering sounds could be heard from the direction of the kitchen. I looked at the alarm clock . . . 3 a.m. Hoping not to wake Kathie I scrambled out of bed, knocked my shin on the bedside table, hopped about a bit in silent agony and, finally, fell backwards on the bed on top of her. Waking with a start, she rolled me off and sat up blinking in the semi-darkness.

'What . . . Is that you, Steve?'

'I'm sorry. I overbalanced.'

'You idiot. What are you doing out of bed?'

'I heard a noise . . . from the kitchen.'

'No. Really?'

'Definitely. I heard the same scrabbling and scampering sounds earlier. That's why I got up.'

'What is it?'

'I don't know but I'm going to find out. I've a torch here.' My eyes had adjusted to the night-time conditions by then and I crept over to the kitchen area before turning the torch on. There, frozen in the torchlight, was a startled mouse with a piece of teacake in its mouth. Instinctively,

I grabbed the small creature which, not unnaturally, did its best to take a chunk out of my hand. Kathie switched the main light on and I dropped the mouse into a large vase on the windowsill, placing a book over the top.

'Are you hurt?' Kathie enquired.

'Just my shin.'

'He can't have bitten your shin!'

I shook my head and laughed. 'Never mind. He's safe in the vase for now. You're not scared of mice, are you?'

'Not at all. I used to have a hamster when I was younger, till . . .'

'What?'

'It was an accident. Someone trod on him.'

'What idiotic numpty—' I began, before realizing Kathie herself was the culprit. Even now, the recollection distressed her. 'Sorry,' I mumbled.

'What shall we do now? We can't leave our friend cooped up in a vase all night.'

'How about the toilet?' I suggested, trying to sound perfectly serious.

'Steve! And you with the RSPCA and all. That's horrible!' She was about to continue in the same vein when, seeing me grin, she realized it was a wind-up and chucked my pillow at me. 'We could keep him as a pet,' she mused. 'Bring him round and tame him.'

Actually, we were in a real dilemma as to what to do with our mouse and I realized it would be a situation that I'd face regularly as an inspector. Basically, it came down to the question: should wild animals ever be kept as pets? Kathie and I talked it over that night and came to the conclusion that, unless there was a compelling reason, the answer surely was no.

'You'll have to sneak downstairs, Steve, and release him outside. We can't have him in here and I don't suppose any of the other residents will want him.' There was a short delay while I put my overcoat on over my pyjamas and unlocked the door. Then, brushing against the banister for support, I carefully negotiated the stairs carrying the bulky vase with the book over the top in front of me. I'd reached the hallway leading to the front door when the light was suddenly switched on behind me.

'What's this then?' barked the hotel manager. 'Stealing our antiques, are you?' I turned round, startled, and nearly dropped the vase. He recognized me instantly. 'Room 35, eh? You're for it, matey. I'm calling the police.'

For a moment, I didn't know what to do or say. Then, recovering, I pointed out that the vase and the book together wouldn't fetch a couple of quid on the market.

'I don't care. It's the principle of the thing. I'm definitely calling the coppers.'

'Okay . . . go ahead. When you're finished I'll use the phone and leave a message for the local Environmental Health department. Take a look in the vase.'

He did, and his face went white. He began to bluster. 'You can't bring pets in here. We're very strict – no pets!'

'I was on my way out, as you know. And this is a wild mouse. Put your finger in that vase anywhere near him if you dare. It was caught in the kitchen area of our room and there are droppings all over the work surface.' Just to pile it on, I added, 'Photographs have been taken!'

I released the little creature outside, hoping his furry coat would keep him warm till he found alternative accommodation, and passed a silent, if fuming, hotel manager on my way back. 'We'll expect a discount next month,' I told him, before rapidly disappearing upstairs.

During the first few weeks of the new year I travelled up to Horsham from Brighton on an early-morning train – enough of a commuter experience to put you off for life. Late, crowded and grubby trains and a sea of glum, staring faces were enough to sour your porridge. Mind you, it was the time of the three-day week with the Heath government at odds with the mineworkers who were working to rule. Together with a global oil crisis, a smile was as hard to find as a lift in a bungalow. There was a rigidly policed speed limit of fifty mph on most roads except motorways which made journeys long and tedious. We tried driving from Brighton to Oldham once but never repeated it. Kathie got a job with the gas board which kept the wolf, if not the mouse, from the door. Equally important, the exams went well, my results ranging from 98 per cent and first in Clinics to 80 per cent and eighth in Humane Slaughter. Together with second place in the important legal exam I was assured of success. However, our numbers had dwindled to just fifteen – one of the class having fainted at the sight of a needle during a training film and a few others deciding the job just wasn't for them after all.

The big day arrived when we'd be told our postings. It was the last day of January 1974 and I hadn't slept a wink the night before. Kathie and I had wondered and speculated about it and even when she finally fell asleep I remained wide awake. It was gone 4 a.m. before I dozed off at intervals but I never really went properly to sleep as such. I had a feeling it would be Walsall but I was perfectly prepared to give it a go anywhere except, maybe, rural Wales. Nothing against the Welsh people, you understand – lovely folk one and all – but, at the end of the day, I wasn't one of them and I could envisage problems real or, more likely, imagined.

It was Tom Wilson, the ex-Navy lad from Portsmouth, who was first into the deputy chief super's office to learn his fate. Left in the classroom the rest of us were laughing and joking nervously, some popping outside for a desperately needed drag. It wasn't long before Tom, a tad disappointed I felt, rejoined us.

'Walsall,' he announced. So much for intuition and sleepless nights, then. Marvin was next and he returned all bright and breezy.

'Well?' I yelled.

'Billingshurst,' he informed us, looking well satisfied with life. It was just down the road from headquarters and a relatively short hop from London, which explained his delight with the posting. I was in next and I left in a daze . . . Accrington, Lancashire.

I sat on my desk dumbfounded while the others trailed in and out of the super's office – some smiling, the majority disgruntled. The luckiest among us, apart from Marvin, was probably Simon Harrison from Manchester who was a member of the hire-car party home at weekends. He got a station just a few miles from his home. There was no doubt who was the unluckiest trainee. It was the end-lessly unfortunate Harry Mellor. He had barely scraped home after a mighty effort in the written exams and his reward was . . . Balham, London. It couldn't have been worse really – a teeming urban area in the capital com-pared to sleepy, genteel Harrogate with its flower shows and spa. Almost certainly, it meant selling his horses and quickly. Harry almost packed it in there and then, but second thoughts prevailed and he decided to carry on after all.

When I discussed the posting that night with Kathie we decided it could have been worse. Apart from Walsall, Enfield and Balham, we'd sidestepped Ipswich, Wolverhampton, Sunderland, Kidderminster and Huddersfield – none of which particularly appealed. Orders of Removal to our stations soon followed and allocations of uniform, drugs, firearms and vans took place in rapid succession. Next, we all lined up for the traditional passing-out parade in the grounds of the manor house headquarters. The executive director performed a plain-clothes Captain Mainwaring-style inspection then hung around long enough for the photo session before disappearing back to his palatial office and comfy executive chair.

That evening a party was arranged at a local pub for the class and the training superintendent to 'let our hair down'.

I pointed out to Len that, thanks to him, I hardly had any left. He said I looked all the better for it and told me to buy him a pint. As ever, he was suave and elegant, exuding style and sangfroid. He also smoked like the old Busk mill chimney back in Oldham all evening long.

Wives and girlfriends were invited and it developed into a grand evening touched by genuine camaraderie and, yes, beer-induced nostalgia. Most of the others sympathized with me almost as much as young Harry Mellor. To them, Accrington sounded dull and depressing and I began to believe them by last orders, though Kathie remained optimistic – perhaps because she'd wisely restricted herself to a couple of vodka and limes all evening. With a flurry of well-meant slaps on the back and firm handshakes we went our separate ways – scheduled to meet as a class for the last time on the morrow.

There was in fact one unexpected outcome of our night out. One of our party was pulled up by Sussex police on the way home. Subsequently, he was banned from driving as he was over the legal limit. He'd been drinking barley wine and that stuff packs a punch. Fortunately, the Society found him a job managing a clinic somewhere down south till his ban expired and he could finally take up his career as an inspector.

It was Friday, 22 February 1974 when Kathie and I moved into the Society's tied house in Accrington which came along with the job. In those days inspectors had to live in property owned by the RSPCA. Quite a few of the yellow General Orders forms we'd signed on our first day at the training school had related to housing matters like decorations and repairs. Suddenly, they became interesting and important.

We met the area travelling superintendent, Bill Watt, outside the property. It was a semi-detached post-war house in a fairly quiet area handy for the shops and the town centre. Back then, all I knew about Accrington was that the football club had gone bust and we'd driven through it on occasional trips to Blackpool during my childhood. Naturally, with my thoughts concentrated on the tower, sandcastles and penny amusements I hadn't taken much notice of anywhere else along the way. Now, like Kathie, I was eager and excited to see where we were going to spend the first few years of our married life. Bill, ominously, seemed embarrassed and apologetic.

'I'm afraid the interior of the house doesn't match its appearance outside,' he announced. 'Still, come inside and take a look round.' He wasn't joking. The whole place needed redecorating and, as mentioned before, there were no handles on the doors, plugs in the sinks or shades on the light bulbs. Most of the tiles on the kitchen walls were broken and in one corner there was a broken, dilapidated old fireplace. There wasn't a carpet or a curtain anywhere but we couldn't help noticing the silver foil cartons perched on all the windowsills – the sort you get with pies from the chip shop. I asked Bill what they were doing there.

'Ah . . . they should have been removed by the council. We had to have the whole house fumigated after Turner left. They put the stuff in those cartons and set it alight. At least you know the place is pest-free.'

'Quite a character, this Turner sounds,' said Kathie.

'Quite. I'm afraid he left under a cloud.' Bill sighed. 'Trouble with the neighbours and a few angry husbands. Between ourselves, Turner was a bit of a ladies' man. He also kept too many animals, a dozen cats and six or seven dogs. Exactly the sort of thing we preach against. There hasn't been time to get the house into shape before you arrived. Get estimates for everything and I'll rush them through the system.'

Tall and lean, Bill was a genuinely likeable bloke in his mid-fifties and I got to respect him a lot over the next few months. You need people who are sympathetic and fair minded in management positions to get the best out of any workforce. I'm not saying he was a soft touch, far from it, just that he had the necessary nous and good qualities to warrant his position – not always the case in the Society as I discovered along the way. I suppose in any large organ-ization some people will inevitably be promoted beyond their capabilities – the Peter Principle – and become, at best, stumbling blocks or, at worst, liabilities. But Bill was first class and helped us a lot in those difficult early days. We had a cup of tea with him and he told me that I'd be the duty officer for the East Lancs and Bolton areas on Sunday – my first day of duty as a qualified inspector. Before he left he said something that has stuck with me over the years: 'This is a busy branch, East Lancs. They must think highly of you to send you here.' Well, I took it as a compliment. But he could have been looking at me and thinking, 'Those blokes at headquarters wouldn't know which end of a horse to hang a nosebag!' Time, as usual, would tell.

# SEVEN

Where to start? In those last few days of February 1974 I didn't know anything about Accrington and Accrington, in fact the whole of my patch of East Lancs, didn't know anything about me. That had to change and quickly if I was to perform my duties with the necessary speed and efficiency. I was to work in tandem with Bolton branch area and when my phone rang at 8 a.m. that first Monday morning it was the newly appointed inspector for Bolton, Ged Hardwick. I'd actually met him briefly in the Midlands during my field training as he was part of Ted Edwards' group. His subsequent posting to Bolton meant that we were both new to our branches and areas. We agreed we would cover one another's area as well as our own on alternate weekends and take every other Thursday as our day off. In the event of an awkward or dangerous job Ged suggested we tackle it together, meeting up at a suitable halfway point between stations. It was all fine by me and, in addition, I accepted Ged and his wife Jenni's invitation to go round with

Kathie for a light supper the next evening. It was a sort of get-to-know-you affair which we all thoroughly enjoyed.

That first morning I recorded a message on my answering machine. It announced that I was usually available to receive calls from 8.15 to 9 a.m., 12.30 to 1 p.m. and 5.15 to 6 p.m. on weekdays. In case of an emergency, the caller was recommended to ring a vet or the police for advice. I had no in-van radio fitted then and couldn't be contacted at other times.

I'd sifted through a long list of jobs handed to me by Bill Watt and decided on a running order for the day. Unfortunately, having looked at a map of my area, I realized I was not ideally positioned. Accrington was about as far to the east of my patch as you could get. In fact, I was right on the border of Rossendale and Jeff Knowles' Bury area. Despite this, Jeff was partnered with the Oldham and Rochdale inspector. It transpired that my home town and our families were just twenty-five miles away – not bad but hardly 'popping round' distance. I thought of Simon from Manchester. Apparently, his mum prepared lunch for him every day and he was out with all his old mates on days and weekends off. Simon and his wife were expecting a new addition to the family and they'd be able to count on all the help they needed from family and friends, which was a real bonus. Then again, I remembered young Harry Mellor, late of Harrogate and now of inner London. All in all, I couldn't really complain.

My first call on that clear frosty day was to see the Lancs East branch secretary, Mrs Hall. She lived in Mellor, an upmarket village on the outskirts of Blackburn, and I met the travelling superintendent at her house. He introduced me to her and we got on well. Angela Hall was an elegant, polite woman in her late forties. Importantly, she made coffee with hardly any milk in it – just how I like it. A biscuit or a sticky bun invariably accompanied the brew, which was no bad thing either. Irritatingly, though, it was Mrs Hall who first made a remark that came to haunt me in the months to come: 'You look very young to be an inspector.' I knew my colleagues were no bunch of old crocks so her remark seemed to suggest she considered I was *too* young. This statement of what seemed to be the general opinion rapidly became a bad joke as far as I was concerned. Similar remarks followed wherever I went. I decided something had to be done, and soon I'd developed a single-sentence reply that was triggered instantly if Mrs Hall's remark or something like it was encountered. 'They're making us younger to last longer,' I'd say, without a trace of a smile. It was arranged that I would meet and report to the branch secretary each week and Bill and I left to go our separate ways.

My next call was in Tockholes near Darwen – an injured bird in the back garden of a bungalow. On the way I'd pulled in to write up my notebook when I noticed a frosted spider's web against a stone wall. Its sheer beauty stopped me in my tracks and I had to get out of the van for a closer look. The cluster of white flakes at its centre and the intricate network of crusted webbing were astonishing. While I was examining the spider's web my gloved hand rested on the stone pillar of a gate and stuck there, the frost being so severe that day. I peeled my glove free like Velcro fastening and returned to the vehicle.

The road to Darwen took me over Oswaldtwistle moors and the views were impressive. I decided there and then that references to the town in my notebook would appear as 'Ossie' to save time, space and possible wrist injury. I learned later that the local name for it was Gobbinland and its citizens were known as Gobbins. They were just the old Lancashire names, now little used, like ours back in Oldham, where we were known as Roughyheads.

Arriving at the address I found that the bird was a starling with a drooping left wing. The position of the break gave me some hope of fixing it and eventually releasing the bird back into the wild. This was heartening news to the woman and her ten-year-old son who had found it. At that time I had no purpose-built boxes for transporting birds and small mammals, and the cat cages or larger boxes were unsuitable as they allowed birds, particularly, to get shaken about and sometimes sustain further damage. I resolved to get hold of some smaller containers as soon as possible.

I'd arrived home for calls and a bite to eat when there was a knock at the door. A young black and white cat, apparently unowned, had been hanging around the caller's house in nearby Midland Street for some weeks. He presented it to me as a stray and the appropriate forms were signed and completed. I had the perfect reason, therefore, to call that afternoon at the branch animal shelter at Altham, just a few miles down the road. Its address was Altham as stated but, seemingly to confuse folk, it was actually in Huncoat, a small village off the Burnley road out of Accrington. Luckily, Bill Watt had mentioned it at our meeting so I found the place easily.

The shelter, with some justification, was the pride and joy of the local branch, who'd built it just a few years before with the aid of a loan from headquarters. The manager at the time was Sylvia Hampson, who ran the place aided and abetted by her dad Alf. Sylvia was unbelievably busy that day and we didn't get much chance to chat. She was slim, good looking, in her late thirties and committed to the care of the animals she and her staff looked after. We always got on well and developed a mutual respect, to the extent that I gave her a lift to the monthly branch meetings and the local vets whenever the shelter van was out of action, which was often. On that first afternoon it was the affable, laid-back Alf who showed me round while Sylvia kept running just to stay still. There were several large kennel blocks for dogs and one for cats plus, outside near the entrance, an isolation block in case of emergencies. A kitchen and destruction room, which brought back memories of Barnes Hill, together with the reception area and a small office completed the layout. Everything was relatively new and pretty state of the art for the time. It was clear from what I'd seen that Sylvia ran a tight ship and the local branch could be proud of the place.

It was then that I made a really greenhorn mistake – asking Sylvia if she had room for my stray cat from

Midland Street. She didn't. However, two cats were due to be rehomed in a couple of days and she'd be able to take him in then, which left me with the problem of finding somewhere to keep the cat in the meantime. Later, when I got to know Sylvia better, I developed a sneaky, exploitative strategy that almost guaranteed success. I found that instead of walking in and asking if there was room for something, I got a much better result if I took the animal in with me or dragged Sylvia out to the van to see it. Blackmailing? Despicable? Out of order? All of those, I agree. But it helped the animals concerned, even if they had to live temporarily in whatever nook or cranny Sylvia could find for them, and it solved what could have been a big problem for yours truly. Sylvia was well aware what I was up to but couldn't help taking the animals in once she was face to face with them. That day, before I'd concocted my cunning plan, I left with my stray cat still in its basket in the van and wondering what to do with him.

I returned home and fixed the starling's wing as best I could in the garage while jobs that seemed urgent just had to wait. It was the kind of pressure, at a much lower level, that I would have to get used to in my busy branch. It just increased over my time as an inspector with the Society, sometimes getting completely out of hand towards the end – but that's a tale for later. I stole a bite to eat and a cup of coffee while watching Kathie tackling the back garden, which had run to seed. Estimates had been submitted to Bill Watt and work on the house would soon start. But the gardens, front and rear, would take a couple of

years or more to turn round. Like a lot of blokes I appreciate a nice garden but hate gardening itself. My contribution
began and ended with mowing the lawn and cutting the
privet and hawthorn hedges that fenced the property
on three sides. Only the border with the house ours was
attached to had wooden fencing then.

I spent the rest of the afternoon tackling a series of jobs
and introducing myself to the local vets and police and
fire stations in the area. Mostly, they were glad to see me
– if only because I'd make their own jobs that bit easier.
Some asked how the last inspector was getting on, but
I gathered they meant Kenneth Levitt not Turner whose
stay had been hectic but short. All I could tell them was
that Levitt had been promoted and posted to the north-
east somewhere.

I returned home that evening exhausted, to hear from
Kathie that Vic Bradley, our neighbour, had called. His two
youngsters had seen me with the black and white stray
cat and they'd persuaded their parents to give it a good
home. I was happy and relieved to accept their offer and
so was Minstrel, as they later called him. I told Vic to keep
him in the house for a while, and gradually introduce him
to the outdoors. It turned out that Minstrel had a stub-
bornly independent streak. He was one of those cats that
like to be stroked and made a fuss off – up to a point.
When he'd had enough a paw with claws half extended
would suddenly land on an arm or a leg and he'd be off on
his travels. He was an expert 'birder' and often returned
with an unwanted present for his new owners which he

deposited on the kitchen floor as if to make up for a show of bad temper earlier. Whatever, Vic's kids loved him to bits so everyone was happy.

The auxiliary secretary for the Blackburn area, Mrs Lloyd, reported the alleged abandonment of a dog in the kitchen of a terraced house in Bonsall Street. Most towns and villages of any size in a branch area have small committees of their own headed by auxiliary secretaries. The RSPCA, very centralist in many ways, has democratic roots that run deep and countrywide.

Abandonments are always difficult and need to be judged on their individual circumstances, which can vary hugely. Arriving at the address, I could see nothing at all at the front and got no reply at the door. Going round the back I found the gate barred so I enquired next door. They knew the owners were away but had seen no one visiting to feed the dog. I shinned over the neighbours' connecting wall and viewed a brown and white terrier cross through the kitchen window. It had a small area of fur loss on its back, probably a flea allergy, but looked in fair bodily condition otherwise. There were food and water bowls on the floor but they were empty. I decided to place Sellotape over the keyholes of the doors, back and front, and leave calling cards to ring me immediately. If I heard nothing in twenty-four hours I would visit again, reassess the situation and try to get food and water to the animal. For prosecution purposes I would need to prove that the dog had not been visited and fed for at least three days.

I left to visit Halfords veterinary surgery in Blackburn,

as I hadn't had a chance to call there before. I knew from the branch books detailing cautions and cases, and from what I'd heard on the grapevine, that the practice was the main supporter of prosecutions in the area, so establishing or continuing a good relationship with them was vitally important. Before any case of cruelty could be assessed by one of the Society's three legal superintendents, an expert witness – namely a veterinary surgeon – must have made a statement to the effect that the animal concerned had been caused substantial unnecessary suffering. Then a formal case form report, containing the statements of all the witnesses involved including the inspector himself, could be submitted to headquarters. Inspectors' statements then featured interviews with the accused as recorded by the inspector at the time or shortly afterwards in his notebook – a distinctly dodgy and unfair system. Not that there was normally any intention to deceive. It was just that, with all the good will in the world, things would be missed and words forgotten or wrongly quoted. Often notebook entries were made in the van after an interview and you'd need to have an elephant's memory to get everything right. The file would also include any photographs taken and other necessary internal forms.

When I started my career with the Society a case file was usually an eighth or, exceptionally, a quarter of an inch thick. When I retired almost thirty years later an average case file was around one and a half inches thick, sometimes a lot more. And today, if anything in the documentation is wrong, not only can the case get thrown out but the inspector can be open to prosecution depending on the circumstances. It seems that offenders' rights are all-important now and the correct paperwork more important than common sense. Sadly, it seems that collectively we have lost the will to properly police and punish those who are beyond the pale.

Once inside the surgery I was introduced to old Henry Halford, the head of the practice.

'Don't worry, young man,' he told me. 'I trained Peter Cameron and all the others since. I'll train you all right. Now, you can ask me or my older son, Barry, for a cruelty certificate or statement but not my younger son, Morris. He's only just out of college. You understand?'

The Peter Cameron he'd mentioned had been an inspector in the area for twenty years or so prior to Levitt and Turner so Henry had clearly been 'training' inspectors for a long time. I presumed the process he referred to was recognizing what was and what wasn't a cruelty case in old Henry's eyes. I wasn't entirely happy with that but decided to reserve judgement for the time being.

A cuppa and a biscuit later I was back on the road again. My next call was at Robinson's Pet Store in Blackburn town centre. Three callers were concerned about a macaw there. I stepped into the shop and there he was in a large cage in the middle of the room. His head was down and he looked pitifully sad and depressed. In addition, he had lost half his feathers. The shopkeeper told me the bird had been like this since the death of her father, who used to look after it as a member of the family. It was in the shop purely as an attraction and not for sale which, in its present state, just didn't make sense. It certainly had plenty of food and water and the cage was remarkably clean. Nevertheless, I was unhappy with the situation. There was a specialist exotic animal vet not thirty miles away who hadn't been consulted. I insisted he be contacted and his advice taken. Also, the cage, though large, wasn't big enough to allow the bird to stretch its wings out fully, which was illegal. It had to be replaced. Withdrawing the bird from public view and the inevitable stress associated with it would benefit him, and I advised he be taken into their private quarters for the time being. I made a point of arranging to visit again in a couple of weeks' time to see if there had been any improvement in his condition.

The injured starling was finally ready for a test flight in the garage and Kathie and I were eager to know whether my efforts had borne fruit. By then he'd been joined in our garage animal hospital by a young pigeon with a damaged wing. Clearly, between my collection of inmates, cages and cat traps and Kathie's gardening gear the RSPCA van was scheduled to see very little of the inside of the garage during its stay in East Lancs.

To our amazement the starling seemed to be flying well indoors and appeared ready to be released. During my lunch break we took him outside in the back garden, both of us excited and hoping for the best. Normally, I would release a bird near where it had been found but Darwen wasn't on my list just then and it wasn't a critical consideration except for birds of prey. Besides, the less time he spent in captivity the better. We took a quick look round to spot any danger and let him go. Unfortunately, his first short flight didn't take him very far and the next thing we knew there was a flash of black and white as Minstrel appeared from his hiding place under a nearby fern. In no time he'd captured the starling and, carrying the bird in his mouth, headed for the roof of the house opposite where we couldn't follow. He was one fit, cunning feline, for sure. Kathie was even more upset than I was and tears were shed. Usually, in such situations, the cat gets the blame for simply following its natural instincts but I won't have any of that. I was 100 per cent to blame and I told Kathie so. I should have made absolutely certain there weren't any cats around. My inexperience had cost the bird its life and I had to own up to that and learn from it – which I did. When I released the pigeon, which was an Accrington resident, a few days later I made sure Kathie was there and that Minstrel and his mates weren't. The bird successfully rejoined the group on the roof of an old lady in Plantation Street who regularly put out food for them.

In the evening I had a call from a Mrs Mason regarding the suspected abandoned dog in Blackburn. She was the owner's sister and was visiting every day to provide food and water and give the dog a run outside. Fair enough; but I told her to get the dog checked by a vet regarding the fur loss on its back, which she was happy to do. Informing the complainant later completed the job.

# EIGHT

There were aspects of my new job that were brilliant. After morning calls I could organize my day and, within the boundaries of common sense, head off anywhere within the branch area. That included much of the Trough of Bowland, an area of outstanding natural beauty covering over three hundred square miles including peat moorland covered in heather and expanses of blanket bog. Rare birds such as hen harriers, ring ouzels and whinchats could be spotted there and, in the valleys and hills, unusual plants like cloudberry, bog rosemary and round-leaved sundew. The area also featured forests and streams, the former ideal for families and picnics and the latter for the children's game of 'cork-racing' which required wellington boots and boundless energy. Though I'd had a radio fitted in the van within a few weeks of my arrival it had been taken out after a short period as the branch felt that it wasn't good value for money and could be included in their ongoing economy drive. No radio in the vehicle meant I wouldn't get calls diverting me all over the place and I'd get a good run at the jobs in my chosen area. Normally, I'd be home for lunch and my calls. If not, Kathie took them for me. The Society got a good deal in those days. With every married inspector there usually came an intelligent, competent wife who worked for it when needed and never cost it a penny.

By late April the brown paper sheeting on the floor was being rolled up and the house looking, at last, more like a home. It was now time to attend my first monthly branch meeting and give the inspector's report. I was invited to call on Miss Potts, the president of Lancashire East branch, at her large detached house in Burnley the day before the ordeal. A spinster, she was a slight, small, busy lady who, unbeknown to me in those early innocent days, had influential contacts at headquarters. It's no exaggeration to say that one phone call and a word in the right ear and I'd have been history in East Lancs. Perhaps it was as well that I didn't know. Don't get me wrong, Miss Potts was perfectly fair minded and willing to give me a chance to shine. In fact she told me that, despite my youth, I came highly recommended by headquarters. I could only wonder who by.

Now, Miss Potts had a large Airedale terrier which, at best, tolerated my presence. On my calling, after a warning bark or two and a quick but embarrassing sniff of my trousers in the crotch area, he usually retired to a favourite window seat and ignored me. It wasn't his given name but I called him Barney – though Barmy would more likely have fitted the bill. Miss Potts, unfortunately, made excessively milky coffee which I always struggled to get down but somehow felt obliged to drink. When she left the room, for whatever reason, I would try to give her aspidistra an unexpected feed but every time I made the attempt Barney would grass on me and start barking on his top note. Eventually I worked out why. He loved the stuff, froth and all, and wanted it for himself. Thereafter, I slipped him regular saucerfuls and we became good friends.

Miss Potts told me I'd be asked questions after my report. Then she'd invite me to leave, allowing the branch members and officials to discuss the rest of the agenda and, no doubt, their new inspector. Before I left I asked her if I could smoke at the meeting, which she assured me wouldn't be a problem as a number of the other members also smoked. It was part of a Baldrick-esque cunning plan to appear less youthful. I'd bought a pipe along the lines of old Ted's at Stafford and, together with an ounce of shag, I hoped to give myself a touch of maturity and gravitas.

I was introduced at the meeting as Inspector Greenhalgh and that was how it stayed for the next twenty-eight years or more. I was proud of my hard-earned position and, while I enjoyed a warm and friendly relationship with individuals and the branch as a whole, I discouraged too much familiarity. In that way I managed to keep my distance from the inevitable scheming and party politics that went on. Overall, I think that I also benefited at the time from a general yearning to return to the days of Peter Cameron, security and stability. There had been upset and upheaval during Turner's watch and, seeing something in me that I'd missed, headquarters clearly thought I'd exercise a calming influence in the branch – as long as I lasted.

I have to admit that standing up and facing the thirty-odd crowd of members and officials to give my first monthly report was intimidating. Like going skinny dipping and finding yourself surrounded by sharks. I was fortunate in that the chairman was a local businessman and kept the sharks – I mean the members – in order or I might have wilted under the tidal wave of questions that followed when I'd finished my report. Everybody, it seemed, wanted a piece of the new inspector and I kept the pipe close to hand or in my mouth long after it had gone out. Somehow I survived, and I'd almost made it to the door and salvation when I heard some bugger say, 'He's a nice enough chap, but a bit young for an inspector.'

One of the worst aspects of the job, of course, was the euthanasia of animals, and running the local Animal Welfare Centre in Cardwell Place, Blackburn, was something I truly loathed. Animal Welfare Centre was a euphemism, of course – it was just another term for a destruction centre. It was as straightforward as that. The thinking behind such places was that owners who might otherwise abandon their animals could take them down to the AWC and have them humanely destroyed at no cost save a voluntary donation. It was a lesser of two evils philosophy and pandered to the worst in people, I think, rather like attempting to combat the huge problem of drugs and the crime they lead to by legalizing them, or responding to the earlier age at

114

which children engage in sex by teaching them about it in primary school. I just don't go along with any of it and I found running the AWC distressing and depressing after a hard day's work. Fortunately, I was just a stand-in for the main man, John Horner, who usually ran the place but was ill at the time. It was an experience I would never have forgotten – even without meeting Karl.

Thursday was open night at the AWC between 6.30 and 8 p.m. That in itself was another daft aspect of it. For the thinking behind the place's existence to be valid it needed wide-ranging opening hours. Prospective abandoners of animals, callous as they must be, are unlikely to be patient or cooperative. They are far more likely to act with selfish impulsiveness than to wait for the one and a half hours a week the centre was open for business. I politely tried to keep my views on the place trickling into influential branch earholes but it was, sadly, a lost cause. The branch and particularly the Blackburn auxiliary, despite its drain on their resources, remained convinced of the AWC's worth and kept it open.

There was usually a steady drip of folk with their animals on Thursdays at the centre. Cats and birds were gradually rendered unconscious and euthanased in chloroform chambers, while the place had a bizarre, almost medieval, machine called an Electrothanator to euthanase dogs. These horrendous walk-in death cabinets were the canine equivalent of the electric chair. After an afternoon's training with one at Rochdale animal home I had a certificate of competence to use the thing, but I never did. The process involved attaching dampened electrodes to a dog's ears and one leg before giving a shock to stun followed by another to kill. It was shocking all right. Often the equipment failed to work properly and the process had to be repeated. The machines stank of burned fur and were poorly designed and maintained. They were, frankly, an abomination and I've never understood why they were approved by the Society. They were gradually phased out of use – though not as quickly as many of us would have liked.

One rainy evening during my period running the centre things had been quiet until a heavy footstep announced the arrival of a man in a tired, scruffy green uniform. He was a self-employed security guard from Rishton and accompanying him was a huge, cross-bred German shepherd-type dog with handsome features, big bright eyes and a thick but dusty black coat.

'This where they put the dogs down?' enquired the visitor.

'Yes, but . . .'

'Here's one for you then. His name's Karl.' He reached forward, trying to hand me the dog's lead.

'Hang on, Mr . . .'

'Tanner.'

'There's a form to fill in before I can accept the animal, Mr Tanner.' He shrugged his shoulders. 'How old is Karl?'

'Eighteen months.'

'Do you use him in your work?'

'What, him? Nah! He's not up to it, see.'

'Anything wrong with him? Does he bite or chase cars?'

'No. Course not. Will this take long? The girlfriend's in the car waitin' for me.'

'So why are you having him put down?'

'I can't be bothered with him no more – not since I met the lass and all. A dog's your best friend, right, but the girlfriend, she's – well, you know.' I gave him a look of pure disgust which he ignored as he quickly signed the form. Then, throwing me the lead, he was off. Karl loyally tried to follow and I had to hold him back. We were left looking at each other, probably with similar emotions of shock, bewilderment and betrayal. He turned and made a sudden move towards me. I was wary of trouble but he simply nuzzled against my leg and stretched out on the floor at my side.

Now I was faced with both a legal and an ethical problem because I knew immediately that I just couldn't destroy this magnificent animal. Legally, I was obliged to carry out the owner's wishes and it would be expected that I'd do so. Then again, Tanner had told me that young Karl was sound and didn't bite or have any other vices. He was simply surplus to requirements in his owner's selfish and self-obsessed world. The large brown pointed ears stretched forward as I set off to get him some water and in an instant he was up and following me. As there was still quarter of an hour till closing time I walked Karl out to the van and opened the rear doors. With a bit of a push I got him in and he virtually filled the space behind the dog guard. I'd done it now. Rightly or wrongly, I wasn't going to destroy this animal.

I had an out-of-hours number for the animal shelter but it was ringing out. I decided Kathie and I would have to accommodate the big feller overnight despite her long-standing allergy to fur. When she saw Karl she fully understood what I'd done and why. We cleaned and brushed his coat and set him up in the little utility room with a warm blanket, food and water. A small electric radiator heated the room so he was comfortable in there. He put his huge front paws on the windowsill, narrowly avoiding a cactus plant, and looked out over the garden. It was still a bit of a wasteland despite numerous trips to the tip, though Kathie's hard work was beginning to show results. A vegetable plot was newly constructed where the foundations of an old greenhouse had been. We'd shifted enough rubble and bricks off that patch of land to fill a large skip and still the odd monster rock would appear, needing two of us to handle it. Money being tight, my dad had bought us a lawnmower which came in handy together with a pair of his old pruning shears and an ancient rake. It all helps when you're young and setting up house on a budget. What Karl made of the view is anyone's guess but he quickly settled down. Before going to bed I took him outside into the garden where he dutifully obliged and, after clearing up, I returned him to his temporary billet. I swear as I gazed into those big eloquent eyes before shutting the door I caught a questioning look, a look that said, 'Will I be seeing you again in the morning?'

Before breakfast next day I rang Sylvia Hampson at the Altham shelter and she was persuaded to take Karl in for rehoming within forty-eight hours. She told me she'd ring when she was ready for me to bring him in and Kathie and I were happy to foster him till then. Kathie had already had a couple of explosive sneezing fits but she was as determined as I was to see Karl get his chance of a new home. In fact, if her allergy hadn't been so debilitating we would have kept him ourselves for sure. I began to see exactly how so many inspectors end up keeping animals they rescue. Inevitably, there's always that pressure to keep the needle in its box and go the extra mile that might lead to a successful result for the animal concerned.

In the few days we had him I took Karl for long walks up the coppice in Accrington. The forested hillside opens out on to flat moorland at the top and it was just the place to romp and play with the family dog. One day someone was flying a kite which had crashed to the ground and Karl took it upon himself to pick it up and return it to me rather than its owner. His head angled to one side and his face wore a puzzled expression as I carried the kite back to the young lad it belonged to. Children, young and older, were drawn to Karl like a magnet. That was fine in itself, as he loved all the attention, but I had to be a bit careful simply because he was a big strong fellow and could bowl me over with no trouble, never mind a youngster.

When I finally handed Karl over at the shelter I was a tad economical with the truth. I told them Tanner's correct name and address but left out all mention of the AWC and the fact that, technically, he'd been signed over to be humanely destroyed. Just to be on the safe side, I emphasized that he mustn't be rehomed anywhere near his old address, though that was already normal practice. Sylvia gave me a long, quizzical look but said nothing. I think she'd twigged that there was something distinctly dodgy going on.

'Thanks, Sylvia.'

'What for?'

'Taking in Karl, of course.'

'I reckon it's me that's been taken in, Inspector Greenhalgh. You're up to something. I just don't know what.' I blew her a kiss and made a quick getaway. If I'd stayed chatting to her I expect she'd have had the truth out of me sooner or later and I wasn't taking the chance.

Karl found a new home within a fortnight. The new owners were the Day family from Barley, a small village near Pendle Hill. They'd converted an old farmhouse up there which had plenty of garden area and was surrounded by rolling hills and great walking country. Just the job for a big, lively family dog full of energy and affection. When animals are rehomed the new owners are never told any previous owner's details and vice versa. It was a sensible rule that avoided trouble and heartache all round and I had good cause to be glad of it then.

A few weeks later I called at the shelter and was met by Sylvia's dad, Alf.

'Have you heard, lad?' I had no idea what he was talking about and said so. 'About Karl.'

'No,' I replied. 'What about him?'

'He's a hero, he is. Saved their lives he did!'

'*What?*'

Sylvia walked in and took up the tale. 'Here.' She handed me that week's edition of the *Nelson Leader*, one of Pendle's local papers. The front page featured a picture of Karl outside a fire-blackened farmhouse. The headline ran KARL SAVES THE DAYS. Apparently, during the night, an electrical fault had triggered a fire in the kitchen of the Days' farmhouse. Karl's beanbag bed was in the adjoining living room and he'd woken to the smell of acrid smoke and the sight of leaping flames at the open door between the two rooms. New fire alarms that worked via connection to the mains had recently been fitted but were not up and working at the time of the fire.

Barking on his top note, the young dog had run upstairs, pushed open Mr and Mrs Day's bedroom door and roused them from their sleep. In double-quick time, the father had fetched their young children and they'd made it down the stairs and outside before the fire could cut off their escape route. An emergency call had alerted the fire brigade who were soon on the scene and had the fire out within half an hour. Karl, however, was suffering from the effects of the smoke he'd inhaled and he tottered and collapsed. He was given oxygen by a fireman and checked later by a vet, who declared him fully recovered. The recently refurbished farmhouse was a burned-out wreck but, thanks to Karl, the family had survived – right down to their two pet hamsters, Blick and Black. I finished reading the article and handed the paper back to Sylvia. She shook her head knowingly.

'I don't know to this day what monkey business you got up to with that Karl,' she said, 'but it seems to have worked out for the best.'

'Cracking dog, eh?' I enthused.

'Good job they chose him. It's not every dog would have done what he did,' chipped in Alf.

'Oh, Sylvia . . . just a sec',' I said, eager to change the subject. 'Come out to the van, will you? I've got two three-month-old kittens you'll love.' As usual, my strategy worked and Sylvia accepted the kittens with a deep sigh of resignation.

'You bugger!' she exclaimed, carrying them away.

'I know . . . but you like me.'

In the van and filling in my notebook I turned on my battery-operated portable cassette player and put on some music – Nick Drake's 'Northern Sky' – and wondered at the sheer timeless beauty of it. In his lifetime Nick's records sold zilch but now you can't watch an evening's television without hearing his music in all types of programmes. I resolved that one day I'd visit Tanworth-in-Arden where he'd lived and pay my respects.

My thoughts inevitably returned to Karl. I knew I'd done the right thing by him but I couldn't help hoping that Tanner would never get to see Karl's picture in the paper or otherwise hear of his incredible exploits. Surely not, though. He'd be too busy with his new girlfriend.

# NINE

Coincidences! We've all got our tales concerning them – some truly amazing, I'd wager. During my long career with the RSPCA I certainly had my share of them. I remember one in particular when I collected a tortoiseshell stray cat from a lady who was getting on in years at Gatty Park, Church, near Accrington. We had a cup of tea together and she regaled me with tales of the cotton mills she'd worked in most of her life. Terrible, noisy places, the old machinery clattering so loud you couldn't hear what some-one standing next to you was saying. Of necessity, people became expert at lip-reading so they could communicate with their fellow workers during the day. In those days ear defenders and the like were just a pipe dream and the wel-fare of workers was not considered. She was a good talker and I ended up staying longer than I'd intended listening to her tales. Finally, bidding her goodbye, I made my way to the animal shelter nearby and was booking the cat in when the phone rang in the adjoining office. No one was available so I answered to help out. It was Stella, the lady from Gatty Park.

'Is that the inspector?'

'Hello. Yes, it's me.'

'I think I must have talked you to distraction, poor man.'

'No, I enjoyed our chat, Mrs Caldwell.'

'Stella. It's Stella.'

'Right.'

'Are you coming back for her soon or will it be later today?' she enquired. I was utterly taken aback.

'Sorry, Mrs . . . I mean Stella. What was that?'

'The cat. Will you be collecting her now or later on? I suppose she escaped, did she, when you were putting the basket in your van?'

'Escaped? Why, no. She's right here in my basket as we speak. I'm just booking her in at the shelter for rehoming.'

'I never had you down as a joker, inspector, and I can't say that I like this one. It's not April the first, is it?' It wasn't, and in any case I would never have dreamt of playing tricks on an elderly lady. I repeated what I'd told her, assuming she'd had an attack of amnesia since my visit.

'But the cat's here – on my lap!' she exclaimed.

'No, Stella. She's here in my basket,' I insisted, looking down just to make sure it wasn't me who was going bonkers. 'Look, I'll come down right away and we can sort this out. I won't be ten minutes.' She was happy with that and rang off. I aborted the booking-in process for the time being and returned to the van with the cat in my basket. This was truly surreal, stone crazy, and I didn't know quite how I'd handle it. I had half a mind to ring Mrs Caldwell's doctor or the local police station, but it seemed a bit over the top. Besides, she'd have to admit she was wrong when I showed her the cat in the basket.

I arrived back at Gatty Park and there was Mrs Caldwell waiting for me in the drive. She had a strange expression on her face, a mixture of relief and consternation.

'I'm sorry about this, inspector. There's been some kind of mix-up.' I nodded and opened the doors of the van. She peered in and got the shock of her life when she saw the tortoiseshell cat in my basket. When it saw her the cat nuzzled its face against the white plastic bars in recognition and affection.

'I don't understand,' she murmured. 'This is not possible.'

'I told you, Stella . . .'

'Come in, will you?' she whispered, in a daze. I marched inside feeling confident and assured – until I saw an identical tortoise-shell cat stretched out in front of her gas fire. The incredible truth finally dawned. She'd actually been feeding two stray cats, both similarly patterned tortoise-shells, without realizing it. We looked at each other and burst out laughing.

'Have they never turned up together?' I asked her.

'No. Never.'

'That in itself is just amazing. You never suspected anything, then?'

She thought for a moment. 'Well . . .'

'Yes?'

'It's just that sometimes I'd feed the cat and not much

125

later it would be back and still ever so hungry. I put it down to worms. That can happen, can't it? All the goodness goes to the worms and the poor cat's still hungry.'

'I see.' I looked closely at the two cats again and they really were incredibly alike – a pair of bookends.

'I'm sorry I doubted you, Stella.'

'Don't apologize. It's just an amazing coincidence, the cats being virtually identical and never putting in an appearance together. How could anyone guess the truth? Tea?' I accepted her offer and made a mental note to remember the incident. After all, one day I might write my autobiography.

Coincidences continued to fascinate me and I remember reading *The Case of the Midwife Toad* by Arthur Koestler. Mostly, the book concerned the battle for acceptance between the different theories of evolution of Lamarck and Darwin, but it had a small section specifically about Dr Paul Kammerer and his researches into coincidence. Kammerer would sit on a bench in the park and note how many people passed by wearing hats and what type and colour they were, or the number of women who were carrying parasols. He soon found that things happened in clusters – perhaps four men wearing identical-type hats would pass by and then none for ages. He suspected that there were actually laws of coincidence, or seriality as he called it – they just hadn't been discovered yet. Fascinating stuff, although it has to be admitted that Kammerer was something of an intellectual and scientific oddball. He even named his daughter Lacerta after Lacertidae, a genus of lizards he much admired.

In my work as an inspector there were periods when examples of Kammerer's cluster phenomenon were very noticeable. I'd never have had a reason to visit a certain street or area and then, within a short period, I'd get three or four calls to that location. Then there were the jobs themselves. I'd be called to rescue a cat which had been stuck up a tree for several days and get two or three similar calls within a fortnight. Afterwards, I might go six or even twelve months without a single cat up a tree to rescue.

There was one coincidence in my career that, coming early on, was particularly unfortunate. Burnley, of course, was in my branch area, which extended along the Todmorden road to the boundary with Halifax area at the tiny village of Portsmouth. I used to puzzle trainees later by telling them that I covered Portsmouth as well as Lancs East and moaning on about jobs at the naval dockyards. Inspectors operated strictly on their own patch in those days and were not allowed to travel outside their branch areas unless their chief or travelling superintendent had authorized the excursion. I was well aware of the rule but I had a mind one day to break it. I'd been working Pendle and Burnley and it seemed silly to drive home for lunch when I intended to carry on there in the afternoon. In addition, I knew that Astins, probably the world's finest pie and strawberry tart shop, was just a few miles down the road in Todmorden, part of the Halifax branch area. Surely, in the circumstances, I could be forgiven for sneaking over the border into Yorkshire for a spot of lunch. I'd gladly pay the extra private mileage incurred.

I'd been visiting Astins pie shop ever since I was a lad and used to come fishing on the canal with my father, who was a member of the Todmorden Fishing Club. The juice that ran from inside Astins' meat pies was pure nectar from the gods, and the heavenly pastry was delightfully crispy on top and deliciously soft elsewhere. I have never – and I mean never – tasted the like before or since. As for the strawberry tarts, it was ditto for the pastry, and the mind-blowingly delicious juice had an intense flavour you'd travel the length of England to experience again. Gourmet nosh up north in Tod – you'd better believe it.

As expected, Astins' shop was packed out and even finding a parking spot nearby presented problems. I'd put a civvy jacket on over my uniform so as not to stand out from the crowd as I queued on the pavement outside. I eventually got served and was carefully piloting my way out of the door, feeling relieved to be on my way at last, when I literally bumped into Bill Watt, the travelling superintendent. Call it coincidence, Murphy's law or whatever but, unbelievably, it had actually happened. At that moment, Bill could have been at home in Preston, down at headquarters in Sussex or anywhere in the whole of the north-west region he presided over, but he had chosen that day and that time to be in Astins' pie shop in Todmorden and caught one of his inspectors AWOL. I just wanted the ground to swallow me up, and I imagined there'd be a severe reprimand or even worse to follow. But, Bill, being a fellow aficionado of Astins, understood the temptation

I had succumbed to and let me off with a quiet word of warning in my ear. Top man, was Bill.

Most working days started with phone calls and paperwork at home – or base as I preferred to call it when writing up my notebook. Then I'd sort out the jobs I'd decided to tackle throughout the day, balancing urgency and location. The following list is typical: injured magpie, Lowergate, Clitheroe; London Smoke Cottages, Knuzden, three feral cats enclosed in garage to be caught and humanely destroyed; Environmental Health department, Blackburn – advise regarding proposed appointment of a dog warden; field, Heys Lane, Blackburn, complaint of horses with no water or shelter; Halfords surgery, Blackburn for results of post-mortem on two dead rabbits; Valley Mills allotments, Nelson, regarding complaint re neglected racing pigeons in dirty shed; Mount Pleasant Street, Darwen, a dog injured and no veterinary treatment; injured hedgehog, Fielding Lane, Ossie; complaint regarding two donkeys with long feet, pens, Miller Fold, Accrington. If one of the complaints turned into a case for prosecution everything else would have to go on the back burner and my time would be dedicated to the collection of evidence and the rescue of the animals concerned.

In spring magpies will gather in large numbers and territorial battles are not uncommon. They chatter like old fishwives and don't mind who or what they disturb. The injured magpie I'd collected was a youngster with a broken leg. When I got home that evening I quickly splinted the leg as best I could before setting off for Blackburn police station where I'd agreed to meet two plain-clothes officers who were engaged on surveillance duties that evening.

'What's it all about?' I asked, at the desk.

'PC Proctor will explain.' I was ushered into an interview room where, to my surprise, Ged Hardwick from Bolton branch was waiting with the constable. He explained that he'd been asked to help out by Bill Watt as the job in prospect was a biggy. With no radios in our vans he hadn't been able to get in touch to let me know.

'What's cooking, then?' I asked, intrigued by the involvement of the bobbies and the term 'biggy'.

'Ever heard of quail fighting?' As my face registered an obvious blank Ged continued, 'There's only been one case before in RSPCA history as far as I know – in Bradford a few years ago. PC Proctor and his colleague PC Gartside believe it's happening now in Blackburn on a regular basis. They've been on obs for several weeks at various addresses in the town. Tonight they've been checking out a cafe in Whalley Range from an unmarked police car and all the signs suggest it's fight time there tonight.'

'Sort of miniature cock fighting then?'

'If you like. It's still a vicious, deadly and illegal so-called sport and we've got a rare chance to crack down hard on it now, working with the police.'

'Cuppa?' asked Proctor. 'Perhaps a snack in the station canteen. You lads might have to wait here a while before we're ready to go in.' That, as far as I was concerned, was just the job. We accepted the invitation and a meal of eggs, chips and beans accompanied by steaming hot mugs of tea.

'These bobbies do themselves well in the food department, I'll say that,' mumbled Ged as another forkful of beans went on the downward path.

'You can say that again,' I agreed, but he couldn't – at least till the next mouthful was dealt with.

While PCs Proctor and Gartside resumed their surveillance of the cafe we finished our meal and were introduced to the other six members of the police team and the man in charge, Inspector Feeley. He explained that the surveillance lads would let us know when to set off for the cafe, where we'd steam in unannounced. We could be there in minutes as the place was only half a mile away from the police station in Northgate. Ged and I would assist in securing the birds and provide suitable containers for their removal. Luckily, Ged had worked with bird experts before, both within our own ranks and with the RSPB, so I could understand Bill Watt's wanting him there with a relative rookie like me, especially on a 'biggy' the like of this one.

It was gone 11 p.m. when the call to action came and Ged and I piled into the back of a police car together with our boxes, notebooks and other assorted items. Undeniably, I felt the adrenaline rush and nervous tension and, even with all his experience, I could see Ged did too.

There were no sirens. We pulled up fifty yards from the cafe and saw the two surveillance lads discreetly looking in the side of the front window. It was hard to believe the owners of the quail would be fighting them on the ground floor at the front of the cafe but, when we burst in on PC Proctor's signal, that's exactly what we found they were doing. Two of the three men present were holding young cock birds and shaking them at each other over the top of a pool table. The police arrested the three men and officially seized the birds. When we examined them it was a shock to find that small, finely honed metal spurs had been attached to their legs and their beaks had been sharpened to cause maximum damage to an opponent. There were seeds and feathers strewn all over the table top and in the runs at the sides of the table where the birds had been kept prior to fighting. Clearly, a crowd had been expected shortly, as a stream of men heading for the cafe turned on their heels after spotting our cars parked nearby. We'd arrived too early to catch everyone involved, but by doing so we'd saved the birds a deal of pain and suffering and still caught the worst offenders. Upstairs, in coloured cloth drawstring bags, were four more birds which looked as though they'd already taken a turn on the pool table. A drawer full of battered cardboard boxes and filthy with droppings was also seized.

Inspector Feeley turned out to be something of a humorist. He questioned one of the arrested men after cautioning him and the man tried to maintain that the quail were for eating not fighting. They had cost twelve pounds each, apparently. I've never forgotten the policeman's dry, sardonic reply: 'Rather dear chicken, isn't it?'

Back at the police station at midnight the six quail were marked and numbered before the Scenes of Crime lads took photographs. All of us involved in the raid ensured our notebook timings tallied before I rang Halfords. A sleepy voice told us to take the birds round to old Henry's house off Preston New Road, Blackburn. It was 1.15 in the morning when Ged and I turned up at the vet's large detached residence. An upstairs window went up before we could knock at the door and Henry Halford, still in his pyjamas, leaned out.

'The front door's open,' he called. 'Give it a good push and put the birds in the hallway, will you?'

Joining us wearing an old brown dressing gown that had seen better days, Henry told us he'd examine each bird thoroughly and make individual notes. We explained the numbering system and were about to leave when his wife arrived with coffee and biscuits. When we left half an hour later I'd changed my view of Henry. In an era when some vets began to operate like shops and getting one of them out after normal hours was like raising the dead, you could always get an answer at Halfords.

It was nearly 2 a.m. when Ged and I went our separate ways. I got the better deal as it was now Saturday and my weekend off. Ged might only get a few hours' sleep before resuming duty. It was a pattern that was to repeat itself over the years – big, long-winded jobs coming in on Fridays just before you were about to clock off. Still, when the call comes you have to be ready to respond. If England or even the mighty Oldham Athletic are playing and you're called out – hard cheese. If you should be setting off on holiday – set off later and lump it. If you're not prepared to put yourself last, you're in the wrong job. That's how it is and probably always will be.

I tried not to wake Kathie when I got home but she's a light sleeper and anyway she was glad to see me home and in one piece. She even got up and made us a cup of tea – true love indeed. We sat up in bed staring at the sky through a chink in the curtains, grateful that if anyone was trying to contact the Society hereabouts the phone would be ringing in Ged's bedroom in Bolton and not ours.

The date of hearing of the quail-fighting case was set very quickly and, in the meantime, Ged looked after the birds. Regular check-ups by Henry Halford were also arranged.

The leg of the young magpie I'd collected had healed well and, as the days went by, his short juvenile tail began to lengthen and his plumage brightened and became quite glossy. We fed him largely on kitchen scraps plus some bird food and the odd bit of fruit. Maggs, as we called him, was quite a character and let you know he was around all right with his constant chattering and demands for attention. When his leg had strengthened sufficiently, he developed the habit of flying on to our heads and refusing to budge until he was offered a tasty morsel by way of bribery and corruption. We knew he was becoming too tame and needed to be introduced back into the wild as soon as possible.

I intended to release Maggs in the Clitheroe area near the house that I'd collected him from but fate intervened and I never got the chance. The latch on the door of the utility room didn't click into place securely after one of us had fed him and with the back door itself slightly ajar

Maggs made a successful bid for freedom. We tried to lure him back indoors or to land on our heads but he was far too intelligent to fall for either stratagem. In the end we had to accept defeat.

'Just ignore him,' I advised Kathie. 'Leave him to his own devices and, hopefully, he'll find his way home. It's only ten miles as the crow flies and he should be all right.' That was okay as far as it went, but unfortunately Maggs didn't think much of that idea. Although we steadfastly refused to react or show any interest in him when we were busy working in the garden, he would fly down and land tantalizingly close by, as if inviting us to try to catch him. Then every time I got in the van and started the engine he'd fly down and land on the bonnet, eyeing me from the safety of the other side of the windscreen with a haughty 'I've got the drop on you, mate' expression. It was, of course, all a game to him but intensely worrying and frustrating for us. This behaviour went on for several weeks and then, one day, he wasn't there. We never saw him again and often wondered what had happened to him. Maybe he'd made it back home or had come to grief in some way. Needless to say, we really missed him and his crazy antics for a long while afterwards. In my mind it emphasized the importance of releasing birds in the area they'd been found and, whenever remotely possible, I did so after that.

By the day of the court hearing in the quail-fighting case there was intense media interest and, as the area inspector who'd reported it, I found myself being interviewed by national newspapers as well as the local variety. Radio

Blackburn, as it was then, also wanted to talk to me. It was my first taste of that sort of publicity and I wondered if I'd come through it unscathed. I remember asking Ged for advice. 'Keep calm and say it as you see it,' he told me. 'And if there's any bugger about with a camera make sure you're wearing your hat. Headquarters are dead picky about that, for some reason.'

Two of the six birds that were seized at the time of the raid had died four weeks afterwards. The vet was of the opinion that delayed shock and stress from their injuries was responsible. The remaining live quail were exhibited in court at the hearing in specially constructed wooden cages. There was some evidence to suggest that the birds had been fed alcohol-soaked corn before being fought. Two of the men involved were found guilty and the charges ranged from using premises for fighting quail to assisting in the fighting of the birds and confining a bird so that it couldn't stretch its wings freely. For good measure the police threw in a charge against the cafe owner of keeping a late-night refreshment house without a licence. As I was leaving court to deal with yet more press interviews I thanked the two officers who had set the ball rolling and done most of the surveillance work. I asked them to keep in touch if they received any reports of dog, quail or cock fighting in the area.

I found handling the press a little easier than I'd anticipated and it was good practice for all the talks I'd soon be giving at the request of organizations like the Round Table and women's groups concerning my work locally and the

Society in general. As the quail-fighting case was rather unusual it made a great impact early on in my career and I smiled when Henry Halford stopped me outside court.

'I told you I'd train you up, lad. You're coming on well!'

# TEN

It was six months into my appointment as the Lancashire East inspector for the RSPCA and I was enjoying life. I'd got to know my patch, the branch members and the shelter staff and I felt I was gradually earning their trust and respect. Headquarters hadn't complained about my paperwork, which was a bonus, and the house had been redecorated from top to bottom and all the necessary repairs completed.

Kathie had got a job with a local travel agent in Blackburn which suited her down to the ground so, at least for the time being, money wasn't a problem. In fact, we even managed a two-week camping break in Folkestone at the beginning of August and had a great time with fine weather, good food and nothing at all to worry us. I vividly remember drinking an expensive Rioja on the beach under a hot sun, accompanied by locally caught prawns and fresh bread. It was that same afternoon that we heard on the radio, an old transistor of my parents', that Richard

Nixon had resigned over the Watergate scandal. It was hard to believe, then, that the President of the United States was actually a crook. Now, of course, it's pretty much expected that politicians will be on the make every which way – a sad indictment of the state of public life. 'Tricky Dicky' turned out to be something of a trailblazer.

We'd been back home for only a few days after our holiday when I had a crash in the van. Ged had been busy in my area while I was away but, even so, quite a few jobs had piled up. My mind was preoccupied with them as I waited behind a smart red Ford Cortina at the traffic lights at Witton, Blackburn. The Cortina signalled left and started to turn in that direction. I intended to go straight on and set off behind him. Unfortunately, a stray dog shot in front of the Cortina, which suddenly came to a halt halfway through the manoeuvre. I piled into the back of him still accelerating. We got out of our vehicles and, much to my relief, neither of us was hurt – just shocked and shaken. Then we examined the damage to the Cortina and my van. The car, which had a towbar on the back, hadn't suffered too much, though the boot was dented. My new van was a tangled mess at the front and the road was littered with bits of metal and broken glass.

As we were exchanging details a bobby arrived, took one look and confirmed my own opinion that my van could not be driven. He arranged for a recovery vehicle and I contacted our transport department which in those days was ably run by just one woman with a secretary. She swiftly arranged for a local garage to tackle the repairs.

Suddenly, the bobby turned from recording the incident in his notebook and put me right on the spot.

'Now then, Inspector Greenhalgh. You can either admit full responsibility for the accident or I shall have to report you. As far as I'm concerned you're one hundred per cent to blame here. What's it to be?' I thought fast. I was well aware that if you ran into the back of a vehicle in front of you it was entirely your fault and I had. Then again, insurance companies emphasized that a driver should never comment on or admit responsibility at the scene of an accident. So it was a straight choice between humouring the insurance company and being reported or honestly admitting liability and keeping a clean licence. It seemed straightforward to me and I fully acknowledged that the accident was my fault.

I took a bus home and spent most of the evening filling in an accident report form which seemed to go on for ever. The damage to the Society's van amounted to a big chunk of the cost of the vehicle when it was new and the accident preyed on my mind. That evening, Kathie baked some absolutely delicious fresh bread and I opened a bottle of my home-made blackberry and damson wine, both of us determined not to let things get us down. Life was just too good otherwise.

One fine spring day I was doing some cat trapping at a farm near Great Mitton on the edge of the Trough of Bowland. On my way over that morning the roads and lanes had been carpeted along the verges with daffodils and dandelions in glorious yellow profusion. Gardeners swear at them and they raise the blood pressure of many, but for a free display of colour announcing the presence of spring and a new order dandelions take the prize. Cherry blossom decorated trees in churchyards and country gardens and magnolias of all varieties were springing to life. We had inherited a type 'stellata' in our back garden which had suddenly burst forth with a fine display of pure white, lightly scented flowers.

Driving through the busy little village of Whalley with its superb abbey and air of monied tranquillity I began to truly appreciate the wonderful landscape of that part of Lancashire, an area that barely gets a mention while everyone sings the praises of North Yorkshire and its coastal towns and villages. For me and many other Lancastrians, here on the edges of 'the Trough' you begin to enter paradise. I thought how lucky Kathie and I were to have an area like the Forest of Bowland just ten miles from where we lived – pretty much on our doorstep, really.

At the Great Mitton farm there were at least twenty feral cats that needed to be caught as the place was being sold for a rural housing development. Most farmers like a few feral or barn cats around to keep down the vermin. Occasionally, I'd even found a place for one or two on farms and avoided having to euthanase them. Generally, though, there was no option as no one wanted them and they could not be handled. Personally, I'd rather deal with a large vicious dog than a feral cat, especially in a small area with limited room to manoeuvre. A dog can only damage you with its teeth while a wild cat has four feet with sharp claws attached as additional armoury. These and the cat's superior mobility make it a formidable opponent.

The farmer at Mitton had enclosed five of the feral cats in a back kitchen that wasn't much bigger than a two-man tent and I didn't fancy the situation. Still, there was a job to be done and I threw myself in along with a grasper and my cat baskets hoping for the best. Inside, it was like the Wall of Death. The terrified cats were throwing themselves around the bare walls in a vain attempt to find a way out and keep what distance they could from me. One by one I managed to secure them on the looped rope of the grasper. Four cats in baskets were quickly and carefully transferred outside to the farmer. Returning to the fray I expected to find the remaining cat still circling the walls as before, but there was no sign of it. Puzzled, I searched everywhere, inside every cupboard, under the stand-up cooker and behind the ancient fridge. No cat was to be seen. I began to think it must have escaped while I was handing over the baskets and I asked the farmer if he'd seen it slip past him. He insisted it was still in the kitchen and went in to look for himself. Drawing a blank, both of us gave it up as a bad job, shut the door and left.

I was halfway back to Accrington when I realized that I'd left my grasper behind at the farm and turned round to go back for it. When I arrived there was no sign of the farmer. I was about to shout and see if I got a response when there was a bang and a clatter followed by a surprised exclamation from the direction of the old kitchen.

'Struth! What the blazes . . .' I recognized the voice of John Mayer, the farmer, and headed over in quick time. Just as I arrived he burst out of the kitchen door, turned on a sixpence and slammed it firmly shut. I stopped in my tracks but didn't say anything as he was obviously too winded to answer. He put his hands on his knees and struggled to catch his breath as he gradually recovered.

'Am I glad to see you back, inspector.' It was then that I noticed blood dripping from a nasty wound on the back of his right hand.

'What's happened?' I asked.

'It's that cat – the one we couldn't find.'

'Looks like you've found it now. But where?'

'You'll never believe it . . .'

'Try me.'

'It was in the blinkin' cooker.'

'No.' I contradicted him. 'I looked under that cooker and it definitely wasn't there.'

'I didn't say under – I said *in* it,' he repeated. This was a real facer. As far as I could remember the door of the thing hadn't been open at any stage and the cat simply couldn't have got inside it. Yet the farmer's statement and his badly bleeding hand were proof positive it had.

'We'd better get that wound tended to right away,' I said.

'Never mind that. I'll see to it. You get yourself in there and catch that banshee once and for all.'

It didn't take long to secure the cat now its hiding place was known, and I rejoined the newly bandaged farmer in the cobbled yard in no time.

'How did it get in the stove?' he asked.

'Ask me another.' I was just as puzzled and bewildered as he was.

'I opened the door automatic like, never expecting it to be there. Next moment, it's up and away and I've got this here leaving present.' Worryingly, a deep red stain was soaking through the thick bandage and it was clear it was a bad bite.

'Better get off to A and E with that, Mr Mayer. You need a tetanus shot and maybe a few stitches. I got a cat scratch about a month ago and my hand ballooned up. I had to get to the doc's pronto.' He nodded reluctantly and resigned himself to a trip to Casualty.

'I'll send a donation in the post,' he said. I gave him the branch secretary's address and told him to make the cheque out to the local branch. Otherwise, headquarters would snaffle the money and my loyalty in that respect was purely to Lancs East now I was stationed there. Later, I found out that his offering was just five pounds. It wouldn't have covered the petrol money, as I had to make four visits to complete the job, never mind anything else. Over the years it was a strange but very noticeable fact that the poorest folk, often in dire straits themselves, generally gave much more generous donations than people who were obviously well off and in a position to give more. Right or not, I used to think that's how the rich folk got rich – a bit of penny-pinching amounting to a deal of pound-saving.

As I mentioned earlier, cats, particularly feral ones, used to be euthanased in metal chloroform chambers. Initially, air holes in the top were left open so that the cats were gradually rendered unconscious by a mixture of chloroform and air. The air holes were then closed, completing what was a deeply unpleasant task. On my return from Mayer's farm I was driving with the van's windows shut. Despite the bright sunshine there was still a nip in the air and it was just a bit too cold for short-sleeved shirts and lightweight trousers. I drove along admiring the awakening countryside, including splashes of bluebells amongst the woods at Spring Wood picnic site, but soon I began to feel sickly and tired. Without my really knowing what was happening the van was swerving to the right in front of a line of traffic coming in the opposite direction. I finally came to a halt at a crazy angle partway up a farm track and it felt as if someone else was driving. I stumbled, almost fell, out of the door and tottered to the side of the track where I collapsed in a heap. By then I had no idea where I was or what was happening. Suddenly, a voice penetrated the mists surrounding me.

'Ho, there. Are you all right, son?' The reassuring tones belonged to a postman tramping back down the potholed track to his van.

'I am now,' I stuttered, beginning to come round.

'I'll call an ambulance if you like. You look fair flummoxed, lad.' Coming from Lancashire I knew he meant

145

flustered and confused and he was right. I was struggling to understand what exactly had happened to me and how I'd ended up on a farm track on the wrong side of the main road. The postie stayed with me for a minute or two till it was clear that I was back to normal, and I thanked him for his time and trouble.

Making my way back to the van I poked my head in at the open door and the strong smell of chloroform hit me straight away, causing me to recoil. I was violently sick in the long grass by the side of the track and it didn't require Sherlock Holmes to solve the mystery now. When I felt up to it, I opened the back doors of the van and checked the chloroform chambers. I found that I hadn't fully closed the air holes in two of them. It had made no difference to the outcome regarding the cats inside but the stuff leaking into the vehicle had got to me and almost caused an accident and fatalities. I knock Health and Safety but a little of it in the seventies wouldn't have gone amiss, I guess. Worse still, I remembered that they'd used carbon tetrachloride in the recent past before chloroform came on the scene. Carbon tet. is almost certainly carcinogenic, inhaling it can be fatal and skin contact can lead to dermatitis. Long-term exposure can result in kidney or liver damage, coma and even death. The move to using chloroform may or may not have improved euthanasia but chloroform is equally dangerous to humans and can cause dizziness, nausea, fatigue and headache, which I can personally vouch for. Chronic exposure can damage the liver and kidneys just as much as Carbon tet. Leaving the doors and windows wide open and closing the air holes of the two chambers eventually cleared the air and I could safely resume my journey home.

Bill Watt had told me on day one that Lancs East was a busy branch and, without doubt, he'd been proved right. Since my appointment the constant flow of complaints, rescues and emergencies had left little time for the important duties at markets and horse fairs in the area. The only long-term solution was to employ a specialist market inspector whose sole duty would be patrolling, in our case, Blackburn and Clitheroe auction marts. It was actually a tricky appointment. The candidate would have to come from a rural, probably farming, background to function effectively in the markets. Then again, they would have to be capable of putting their foot down when necessary and insisting standards were kept high and the legislation on the welfare of animals was respected. In addition, a good relationship needed to be established with the auctioneers and any Ministry vets attending the sales. It was something of a balancing act and finding the right man would be difficult. Fortunately, things worked out well.

Bert Swinbourne came from a farming background and lived in the pretty village of Waddington near Clitheroe. His cottage was straight out of a country-life magazine: pure chocolate box with a narrow bridge over a slow-running stream outside his front gate. Waddington itself is one of the prettiest villages you'll ever see and has won the Lancashire 'Best Kept Village' contest many times. It's also known for its scarecrow festival each May and regularly hosts stream-driven duck races, of the plastic variety, for charity. Bert was a smashing bloke, around sixty years old, medium height, grey flat cap and dressed by Greenwoods. He was just right for the job and a real character as well. The first time I called on him he asked if I'd mind taking my boots off as a new living-room carpet had just been fitted. I readily obliged. Seven years later I was still going bootless in Bert's front room and, to be fair, the carpet still looked as good as new.

'Carpets is damned expensive!' he'd proclaim, every time we entered the room. This was usually followed by, 'An' this 'un will see me out, I'll be blowed.' He offered me a glass of his home-made wine, which I gratefully downed, and we ended up discussing our mutual interest in the subject for the next half-hour.

'It's all to do with the right yeast,' he said, pouring us both a second glass of peach and dandelion, an unusual combination he much favoured.

We drove over to Clitheroe market later that first afternoon and I introduced him to all and sundry, some of whom he recognized as casual acquaintances. He impressed me with his keen eye, easy manner and, importantly, his knowledge of the legislation. He spotted that one of the pens was overcrowded and contained both horned and unhorned cattle. They needed separating to ease numbers and avoid injuries. We went in to help remove the animals with no horns to a nearby empty pen. In the restricted space a bucket of water got in my way and my foot knocked against it. To my surprise I staggered to one side, struggling to keep my balance, and one of the animals promptly stood on my outstretched foot. Even with a protected toecap it was a painful experience. When we'd finished the job Bert accompanied me as I retired hurt to the van. Just the slightest of grins was detectable on his wrinkled face.

'You might think it's funny, Bert . . .'

'No . . . not funny exactly.'

'That was one hefty beast.'

'Aye. But you seemed a mite unsteady, Steve.'

'You're right. Actually, I still do.'

Bert grinned. 'It's the old peach and dandy, I'm afraid. Happen that second glass was a mistake. If you're not used to it, well . . .'

'Too true,' I agreed.

'I was just bein' polite like. Never havin' met you before.'

'I'll know better next time . . . It's all in the right yeast, did you say?'

'Aye.'

I quickly got to know Bert well and within a few weeks I felt confident enough to leave him alone in the markets. Besides, because of his other hobby, it cost me money every time we met. When he wasn't working Bert was a regular at the antique fairs and general sales around the area. He prided himself on 'buying cheap and selling strong' as he put it. That was fine as long as you weren't the one buying from him. Somehow, he managed to sell me something I didn't like and didn't want whenever we were together.

He was a real-life Auntie Wainwright, straight out of *Last of the Summer Wine*. I still have no idea how he did it. I reckon not to be a soft touch in that direction, but Bert generally made mincemeat of my puny efforts to avoid a purchase. I acquired a whole range of dubious items including two rickety Victorian table chairs, a faded water-colour by an unrecognized artist of Hodder Bridge, near Clitheroe, and a small Beswick figure of a cocker spaniel with a hairline crack. All of them were a tribute to Bargain Bert, as I christened him and his persuasive tongue. Kathie used to go mad when I arrived home with yet another naff or knackered item after a visit to Waddington.

Having got thoroughly fed up over the years, I finally refused to buy another picture Bert showed me. It was a small, dingy, dark grey canvas populated with ghostly figures. It had all the appeal of Michael Barrymore's swimming pool on a humid evening in Harlow. To be honest, it looked in urgent need of a final resting place on the nearest landfill site.

'I don't want you to buy this, Steve. Times is hard and all that . . . an' you and your missus having a young 'un soon.' On my last visit I'd let slip that Kathie and I were starting a family. Bert was overjoyed, although I don't think that he and his wife, Marjorie, had children of their own.

'I bought this for your expected,' he continued. 'It should be worth a penny or two after bein' restored.'

'That's really thoughtful of you, Bert. And don't think I'm ungrateful, but . . . that picture looks in bad shape. Is it really worth anything?'

'Wot, this? A Major? I paid . . . well, never mind what I paid. It's worth twice as much just as it is.'

'You're sure?'

'Trust me. It's a Theodore Major. Most folk at the sale took one look and didn't bother. The only other chap biddin' seemed half hearted too. Probably the condition told agin it.'

'I'm not surprised. Still, it's really good of you to think of doing this and you've never been wrong that I know of, so . . .'

'Trust me,' he repeated. 'When's your young 'un due?'

'November. Middle of the month.'

'I'll have the Major ready by then. Count on it.'

We had just half a glass of Bert's delicious three-year-old rosehip wine to mark the gift before I was on my way again.

I was surely but slowly developing useful contacts across my patch and Bert was certainly one of them. He was a mine of information about the farming community and even, on occasion, had information on dog fighting and the like. The branch had certainly struck lucky when they appointed Bert as their market man.

In the early hours of a freezing cold November's day a few years into my service as an RSPCA inspector in Lancs East branch Kathie and I were blessed with 'a beautiful baby daughter' – the doctor's words when he summoned me from a waiting room at Queens Park Hospital, Blackburn. I'd been with Kathie most of the time till I was ordered out of the room when things got a bit hectic near the end. The doc was spot on with his description and while Kathie held her I presented our newborn with a single red rose to mark her birthday.

Outside, through the window, pale yellow lights streaked the darkness and revealed flurries of snow being blown about by the wind. Inside, we were warm and so very happy. I can honestly say it was the best time of my life and I seemed to be floating on air. My hands were shaking when I held our daughter in my arms for the first time. I wasn't afraid of dropping her or anything like that – it was the sudden, awesome responsibility of being a father that almost overwhelmed me. Kathie sensed it and said she knew I'd be a brilliant dad. I wasn't so sure but I was certainly going to try.

A few days after the birth Bert turned up on the doorstep with the restored painting and left it with me. The transformation was miraculous and later we put it away safely for our daughter, Emma Kate, till she could appreciate it. Since, I've been offered fifteen hundred pounds for it and the current valuation, 'bein' a Major an' all' as Bert would say, is two thousand plus. I got to know that Bert had paid just fifty for it at the auction. Once again, he'd been right and lived up to the name I'd given him. To this day I always remember that act of pure unexpected generosity whenever my own home-made wine accompanies our Sunday dinner.

# ELEVEN

It's generally perceived that the RSPCA is more or less akin to the police force, staffed on similar lines and run on taxpayers' money. Nothing could be further from the truth. It's probably true to say the Society itself has aided and abetted the misconception through advertising that emphasizes twenty-four-hour coverage. Such coverage has only been achieved by inspectors who have worked a full shift during the day and continuing, on a rota basis of late, to undertake duties at night and weekends. The dedication of the Society's Inspectorate to duty and the cause of animal welfare has meant that twenty-four-hour coverage for urgent and emergency calls has been the norm. In addition, being known as the 'animal police' has fostered the idea of immediate response and availability in the public mind.

Some folk used to come on the phone convinced they were ringing a large office packed with call reception staff and hordes of inspectors loafing about waiting for something to do. I usually tried to put them right but sometimes it was tempting to go with the flow and deal with the caller's expectations in a more mischievous way. One morning the phone rang at 8 a.m. Unfortunately, I was upstairs shaving at the time and I trailed a long line of white foam across the new stair carpet as I padded across the landing to reach the phone in the bedroom. Kathie gave me an angry glare.

'Hello,' I gurgled breathlessly.

'Is this the right number?' queried the unimpressed, rather posh voice on the other end of the line. 'I want the RSPCA office.' Kathie started to dab at the shaving foam decorating my face with a towel from the airing cupboard.

'Yes, it's the RSPCA. Can I help?' I spluttered, scattering foam everywhere and trying desperately to dodge Kathie's helping hand.

'Montague Grierson here. I'm a JP, Ribble Valley area. I . . .'

'Will you leave off!' I yelled, the end of the towel flapping over my mouth.

'I beg your pardon?'

'No . . . not you. I mean *you!*' I somehow managed to escape Kathie's clutches behind the bathroom door. By then, the exasperated JP's patience had run out.

'What's the meaning of this . . . this outrageous behaviour? Am I speaking to the inspector or some drunken lunatic?' Keeping calm, I managed to convince the caller I was both sane and sober and the inspector he expected on

154

the end of the line. Eventually, a placated Monty got round to what the problem was.

'Eleanor's pussy has gone missing. Since seven o'clock last night. She's doctored and never goes out after tea as a rule. I can't understand it and Eleanor, my wife, is just devastated.'

'I see. Has she ever strayed before?' I enquired.

'Certainly not. It . . . I mean Meisha keeps herself to herself. A very clean cat too, always licking her fur. Independent, though. She doesn't like being handled or picked up. Occasionally, if she's in the mood, she'll let you cuddle her.'

'What, er, colour is Meisha?'

'Black and white.'

'Any distinguishing features?'

Monty thought for a moment. 'Lovely loud purr, Meisha has. Unmistakable.'

'Nothing else?'

'No. Not that comes to mind. You'll be starting the search for her directly, I assume.'

Initiating a neighbourhood search for a black and white cat with a loud purr missing for one night in an area of vast fields and great tracts of woodland when I had a fistful of urgent complaints and several injured animals awaiting collection was, to say the least, simply not on. I puzzled for an answer – how to puncture Monty's absurdly high expectations and remain on speaking terms? After all, he might well be judging one of my cases in future. The plummy voice on the phone started up again . . . 'Hello? Look here. When can we expect you?'

'Er, Mon— I mean, Mr Grierson.'

'Ah, you're still there.'

'Yes. Look, we're a bit short handed at the moment and it will take a while to organize a search team, but in the meantime I'll send round my best man to see how the land lies, work out an effective strategy and all that.'

'Very well.'

'And don't worry. This chap's first class – one of our high-flyers. He'll find Meisha if anyone can. Will ten o'clock this morning suit?'

'Certainly. We'll expect you then. Goodbye.' I returned to the bedroom, put the phone down and shook my head. Another blob of shaving foam took off and landed on my Rolf Harris LP. I immediately cleaned it off. I've a soft spot for Rolf and all his works but any musical credibility I had amongst my friends would have evaporated instantly if they'd known. My 'tie me down' addiction had to remain a deep, dark secret. Consequently, not for him a place amongst my Pink Floyds, Caravans and Van der Graaf Generators in the living room but a hidey-hole just behind the bed upstairs. Good old Rolfie . . . I still think his version of 'Stairway to Heaven' put Led Zep's to shame. Eat your hearts out Planty and Page.

I reckoned I could fit Monty into my morning schedule as I had an injured racing pigeon to collect in Chatburn, which wasn't far from Chez Monty in Downham. Much to my surprise, when I called, he had gone out on business, leaving Mrs Monty, the devastated Eleanor, to deal with me. The lady was certainly distraught and could hardly string a sentence together as she marched back and forth across the expensive Axminster wringing her hands in despair. A maid arrived with tea and biscuits and I was admiring the wisteria along the garden wall when a slim, elegant, black and white feline strolled across the lawn towards us. Mrs Monty had just sipped some of the smoky-flavoured Lapsang Souchong we'd been served when she caught a glimpse of the cat. She spluttered and choked at the unexpected sight – as positive an identification as you could wish for.

'Meisha!' she squealed. 'It's dear Meisha come back to us.' She rushed outside, theatrically swept the bewildered, struggling cat up into her arms and, as she re-entered the house, subjected her pet to a stern cross-examination. 'Oh, Meish . . . where have you been? Have you been trapped somewhere, perhaps kidnapped and escaped? Look at your fur, it's all wet and tangled. Are you hungry? How could you wander when you have all you need here? Still, thank good-ness, you're back.' While I was pleased that Mrs Monty's pride and joy had returned so unexpectedly I couldn't help feeling that I was trapped in some third-rate amateur dra-matic production listening to the heroine's heartbreaking, over-the-top soliloquy. As for Meisha, the cat seemed fine to me and a small area of mud-caked fur on one side at her rear was really nothing to worry about. I left the tea and biscuits untouched and departed in haste. There was no word of thanks and, more important, no donation.

As I passed the gleaming Bentley in the drive on my way out I was reminded of the week I'd spent at Kilburn clinic in London during training. The clinic was supposed to cater for people unable to afford veterinary treatment for their pets. On a coffee break one morning I looked out of the window and saw a chap in a Porsche park in a side street. He turned up in reception a few minutes later with his pedigree Labrador retriever lame on a back leg. The veterinary nurses confirmed that it wasn't an isolated incident – more like a daily occurrence. Ah, well . . . cheapskates will always be with us.

It wasn't long after the affair of the Montys and their 'missing' Miesha that I had a cluster of jobs in the fashion of Kammerer's coincidences. I received three 'bird calls' in quick succession. The first was from Blackburn police at 7.30 a.m. one day. A swan had crash-landed in the middle of Bolton Road outside the Royal Infirmary. It was a busy main road and an officer had been sent to deal with the call but now he was requesting RSPCA assistance. I asked if the swan was injured.

'He's not sure,' answered the voice on the phone. 'But it soon will be with rush hour approaching and no sign of it moving.'

'I'll be there in twenty minutes,' I assured him and washed and dressed quickly. Before setting off I emptied the back of the van of some equipment and spread thick layers of newspaper behind the dog guard in case I had to transport the bird.

I arrived on time and met up with PC Aitchison. I noticed that he was standing well clear of the swan, a large cob, which had sat down to rest on the white line in the middle of the road and seemed to like it there. The bobby seemed more than pleased to see me.

'Ah, inspector. Glad you've arrived. He's a big lad is this fellow.'

'Have you seen him walking about?'

'Yes. He could walk all right but his left wing seemed to be hanging a bit low so it might be injured. I couldn't tell for sure.' I could see there was no blood around on the road or on the bird itself, which was all to the good. Nevertheless, one of the wings could have been damaged by contact with an overhead wire or on landing. Until I got a grip on him there was no telling. I returned to my van for the screw-together wooden rods and swan hook only to find that I'd not put them back after laying down the newspapers. I would just have to tackle the bird unaided. Going home for them wasn't an option as the traffic was already increasing and PC Aitchison was keen to be on his way.

I approached slowly, adopting a nonchalant aspect, but when I was around five or six feet away the swan looked me hard in the eye and stood up with his wings arched over his back. A snort and a hiss emphasized that he regarded me as a threat and was prepared to give me all the trouble I wanted and then some.

He stood his ground and waited for my first move, which was to ask PC Aitchison to spread his arms out and prevent the bird from making a run for it to the hospital side of the road while I made a grab for its neck. I missed my target and the policeman's presence didn't deter the cob in the least. He paddled along at a great rate, wings outstretched, straight at the bobby whose nerve, not surprisingly, broke. He dived to one side like an England keeper when we used to have good ones like Ron Springett and Gordon Banks and just avoided a collision. The bird's left wing scraped his ankles as it passed by.

'Are you okay?' I enquired, helping him to his feet.

'Oh, aye,' he said unconvincingly. As he brushed his uniform down I could see that he was absolutely terrified of tackling the swan again but determined to give it another go anyway. That, for me, is the sign of a bloke with some backbone. Going back and facing something when every instinct is telling you to do the opposite is what courage is really about and PC Aitchison had it. He'd probably tangled with some real hard cases in his time on the force without thinking too much about it but now, out of his comfort zone dealing with a belligerent swan, he was finding it hard work. Maybe I sympathized with him so much because I had some demons of my own to face – I don't know.

Leaving the constable, I stepped across to the side of the road where the swan was sitting keeping a watchful eye out. He was about to rise and adopt the wings-back posture as before when a dog approached him from the pavement. The bird's attention was momentarily diverted and I rushed forward, grabbed his neck and wrapped my arms securely round both wings. He hissed and put up a tremendous struggle to get free, but by the time I'd reached the van and deposited him safely inside he'd calmed down a lot and seemed to accept his fate. When I turned round the bobby's mouth was open and his jaw heading for the floor.

'You all right?'

'Fine,' he replied, shaking his head. 'That was brilliant – the way you handled that swan. I'd still be here next week trying to catch him.'

I laughed. 'It's not so difficult when you're used to it. Each to their own, eh?'

'Thanks, anyway.'

I took the swan to the nearest vets, Carrier and Grant, to minimize travelling time which could aggravate or worsen an injury. Mr Grant examined the bird while I held him securely. Fortunately there were no injuries, and I released the swan immediately on a quiet stretch of the Leeds & Liverpool canal nearby. His landing in the middle of busy Bolton Road was probably through tiredness, though he may have been en route to Ewood Park to watch the football and had second thoughts.

My next 'bird call', a few days later, saw me heading in the opposite direction – to the College of Education in Burnley off Colne Road. The place was shut for the holidays and I couldn't get in at any of the main entrances. Finding a couple of telephone numbers in the Yellow Pages I rang them from a phone box that surprisingly, given its location, hadn't been vandalized. There was no reply on either of them and I seemed to have hit a brick wall. How could I rescue the reported injured pigeon on top of a large tower block if I couldn't gain entry to the building? I thought of involving the Fire Brigade but we were locked out, there were four tower blocks to choose from and the caller hadn't left any contact details. I couldn't see a thing from the ground that would help solve the problem. As I was about to call time on the job, there was a heavy tap on the window of the van and I lowered it a few inches.

'Have you come about the pigeon?' At first I thought it was the caller but it turned out to be the college caretaker. He said he'd been on his dinner hour which I took with the proverbial pinch of salt as it was three o'clock in the afternoon and he smelt strongly of Carlsberg special.

'Have you seen it?' I asked.

'No. A woman knocked on the door earlier and reported it. It's on the roof of the central tower block over there. I was going to ring you but I couldn't find your number in the book.' I let that go as, in his state, he might well have had trouble turning the thin flimsy pages. We finally got inside the college and, small cardboard bird carrier in hand, I headed for the lifts.

'Where are you going?' enquired the caretaker.

'To the lifts.'

'That's no good.'

'What do you mean, no good?'

'They're off when the college is closed.' That stopped me in my tracks.

'Can't you put them back on temporarily while I rescue the bird?'

'Nay! No, nay, never, lad. More'n my job's worth.'

I'll always remember that walk up those endless stairs. It was bad enough in itself climbing so many storeys, but having to stop after each one while the portly caretaker gulped in fresh air and swayed ominously from side to side turned a slog into a nightmare. Unbelievably, when we reached the top he found he'd forgotten the key to the door giving access to the roof area. I slumped wearily to the dusty concrete floor as his slow, heavy footsteps receded into the distance below. I reached into my pocket for my pipe then realized I'd left my lighter at home. The long minutes snailed by and I wondered if he was coming back at all. I noted the legend 'Kilroy wuz here' inscribed on the wall. I wondered if there was anywhere Kilroy hadn't been? He was probably the most travelled man on the planet.

The tipsy caretaker took over twenty minutes to return and looked like a candidate for the mortuary. His face was as red as a beetroot, his nose redder still. He took great gulps of the stale air and sat down on the landing to recover. I seriously thought that some sort of medical emergency might develop.

'Take your time, mate,' I told him, 'there's no rush. You look done in.'

'It's the fags!' he exclaimed, in a single burst of breath. Even those few words seemed to require a Herculean effort on his part.

'You want to give them up. High blood pressure too, have you?'

He nodded. 'I take pills!' he wheezed, recovering a little.

'Got any on you?'

'It's all right. I took one before I set off back up these stairs.' With an almighty effort, the fellow got to his feet and staggered over to the access door before feeling in his pocket for the elusive key. Finding it, he inserted it in the lock and tried to turn it – without success. 'It's been a while since anyone's been up here,' he explained. 'Don't worry. It's definitely the right key.' He put pressure on the key as he twisted it. Sweat appeared on his brow and a red mist of manic determination set into his face.

*Snap!* The half of the key in the lock suddenly parted company with the half in the caretaker's hand. He nearly fell over again – just about keeping his feet at the parting. I examined the keyhole of the door.

'It's a locksmith's job now,' I told him. 'You'll have to get one out right away.'

An hour and a half later we finally gained access to the promised land of the tower-block roof and the locksmith packed his bags and went on his way. The flat roof covered a large area and I expected it would be difficult to spot a pigeon at first. In the event, I never spotted one at all. The 'pigeon' turned out to be a swan and very easily located by the lift shaft. As I stood there with a small cardboard bird box in hand staring in disbelief at the erstwhile pigeon I began to feel rather foolish. Some calls the Society receives are short on detail or, as happened with the horse complaint in Peterborough, the location is vague but how, I wondered, could someone mistake a swan for a pigeon? It defied all sense and logic but there it was – someone had.

I handed the bird box to the caretaker and slowly, from

an angle, approached the swan which was looking at me suspiciously. I noticed blood was dripping from a wound on her breast and her head was nodding intermittently. It was dismaying to see such a beautiful creature wounded and virtually helpless. Nevertheless, I cut off her escape route to the edge of the roof as much as possible and stepped forward stealthily and briskly. I expected some fireworks but the pen was clearly too weak for that. She let me capture her and struggled very little all the way down the flights of stairs to the ground.

I realized things were touch and go with her. Birds in general resent handling by humans and can quite rapidly deteriorate and die from shock. I quickly transferred her to my van and left behind the exhausted caretaker who, no doubt, was glad to see the back of both of us. I drove to Hartley and Owen, the vets just round the corner. It was the start of evening surgery and the place was heaving but the receptionist ushered me straight through to a consulting room where Gerry Owen, one of the partners in the practice, was washing down the examination table and disinfecting after the last patient.

'Hello, Steve. She's a beauty you've got there. Put her on the table.'

'It's a wound on her breast, Gerry. Likely she's hit an overhead electricity line. There may be other injuries. It didn't seem sensible to examine her and add to the shock when the practice was nearby.' He checked the bird over and tended to the dark, scorched wound disfiguring her otherwise regal appearance.

'The good news is she's no other injuries, Steve. The wings are normally positioned and working as they should, along with the head, neck and legs. I think you're right about the overhead line – probably a glancing blow from below rather than a full-on collision. As you know, they're usually fatal or result in really terrible injuries. Leave her with us and we'll contact you soon with a progress report.

The swan survived all the handling and the shock of her ordeal. Following a period of rest and recuperation at the Altham shelter, I released her on a lake in the Burnley area where she found a partner and produced five beautiful, grey, fluffy coated cygnets later that year. It was the kind of result you dream of and makes everything worthwhile. You feel as if you've made a real difference and when it comes to job satisfaction it doesn't get much better than that.

The third memorable 'bird call' in quick succession came when I was called out to Hagg Lodge off Hyndburn Road in Accrington. The lodge was used by a local fishing club and had featured on my radar several times before. I expected to find a bird tangled in discarded fishing line, or one that had swallowed line and maybe a hook with it. It turned out to be more dramatic than that. A male mallard had been seen on the water with a crossbow bolt piercing its left wing.

As an RSPCA inspector you necessarily witness the results of all kinds of viciousness, neglect and cruelty to all kinds of animals, domestic and wild. Inspectors aren't easily thrown off kilter by such incidents and tend to knuckle down to resolving the immediate situation and finding the way forward. Perhaps later, the adrenaline still pumping but easing off, there might be time to consider and reflect but all too often there's another emergency to deal with and it's back in the van to scour the street maps for the new location. Nevertheless, when I drove down to Hagg Lodge and walked three quarters of the way round before spotting the bird on the water I was both stunned and moved. The sight of the bolt penetrating the drake's wing was pitiful – a product of mindless, morbid stupidity at best and something deeper and darker at worst. You see both sides of the human condition on a regular basis in the job and I suppose it's not surprising that some people eventually get burned out, as they say. Yet I knew the good far outweighed the bad and I strongly believe it still does.

Over the next few days I tried all the usual tricks to catch the duck from the bank but nothing came close to working. It soon became clear that I needed help, and a boat would undoubtedly come in handy too. After taking lunchtime calls I rang Ged Hardwick in Bolton who agreed to come over to Accrington the next day with a boat borrowed from the Manchester lads. Luckily, he'd recently had a tow bar fitted to his van at his own expense as he'd bought what he called a 'mobile home'. It was actually a beat-up old caravan even old man Steptoe might have walked away from. Ged couldn't see it, though. To him, his new acquisition was a thing of beauty to be gazed at and admired by all who set eyes on her. When he invited me over to take a look I found it difficult not to laugh.

'Brill, isn't she?' he chirped. It was one of those questions best answered by a nod of the head, which I somehow managed with a straight face.

'Classic lines, hasn't she?' he continued. 'They don't make 'em like her any more.' I could only nod again in agreement and rejoice in the advances in 'mobile home' technology.

'Course, she needs a bit of restoration work – a touch here and there,' he admitted. I nearly blurted out that he must be touched buying the thing in the first place but, somehow, I kept schtum.

'Twenty years old – though you'd never know it,' he went on. 'Not many of her class left, as the salesman said.' I yearned to ask 'What class?' Surely it was obvious why there weren't many left – they'd all rotted away or fallen victim to the scrapyard crusher. Still, silence is golden and I walked away without a wrong word said – a saint in the making.

The next day I met Ged at Hagg Lodge which he knew well, having been called out there several times himself when he'd been covering my area.

'How's the old caravan then?' I asked him, a slight smirk on my face.

'Not so much of the old, mate. In her case, age is beauty.'

'Done any work on her yet?' I asked innocently.

'I've knocked out that bit of a dent over the offside wheel arch. Some filler's fixed her up champion.'

'Any leaks that you've noticed?'

'Well, there are problems with the windows but they'll fix fine.'

'Good. Glad to hear it.'

He gave me an 'I know what you're really thinking' look, swiftly followed by a lecture on repairing and restoring caravans or, as he insisted, mobile homes. With some difficulty, I turned the conversation round to the injured duck and the job in hand. We tried catching him from the bank but as soon as he spotted our nets he was off and no amount of Mother's Pride would get him to come near us again. In all probability he'd been caught before and this, together with the crossbow incident, meant any trust in humans had evaporated completely.

'Right,' said Ged. 'Let's get the boat out then.'

'Good job it's an inflatable. There's no slipway here or anywhere else you could launch a rigid type.' The lodge itself was twice the length of a football field and at least as wide as one, giving the duck, despite his injuries, plenty of room for manoeuvre. We put on our boiler suits and life jackets and clambered aboard. The boat had an outboard engine but Ged was reluctant to use it until we were well away from the bank and the shallow water and weeds.

'Right, Steve. You take the wheel and I'll fire her up.'

'Okay.'

What is it with outboard motors? Is there one, just a single one on the planet, that starts up first time? If there is, I for one have never come across it, or met anyone who has. Events tend to follow a set, similar pattern. First few attempts, nothing; next couple the odd 'phut' or two; then, third time round, a promising 'phut, phut, phut' followed by a stall. At this point the exasperated bloke (rarely a woman as they have more sense) usually announces, 'There must be some water in it.' He takes a break and gulps in fresh air. Sufficiently recovered, he goes for it big time, pulling on the line for all he's worth and toppling backwards in an inglorious heap. Bruised and battered, he's rewarded by a tigerish purr of the motor – running at last. This was pretty much the way of it when Ged started our outboard that day and we headed for the duck in the middle of the lodge. Handing over the wheel to Ged, I was poised with the net, ready to pounce and secure the bird if the chance came my way.

As we reached a point some fifteen to twenty yards away Ged cut the engine and we drifted slowly forward towards our target, while the bird eyed us with a mixture of curiosity and consternation. Then, as I readied myself to scoop him into the net, he dived under the water and disappeared. We scanned the waters for him but there was nothing to be seen for a while. Then Ged spotted him coming to the surface some thirty yards away.

'There. There he is.'

'Where?'

'Over there . . . to the left.'

'Port?'

'Nah . . . gives me gout. But we'll have a pint in the Plough afterwards, eh?' I slowly shook my head and told him to bring the boat round forty-five degrees. The duck headed for the side of the lodge as we tagged along behind. Closing in, it looked as if we'd got him for sure but at the last moment he pulled the same diving dodge as before, disappearing below the murky grey water and resurfacing a good distance away – this time behind us.

'He's making mugs of us, Steve.'

'It's one heck of a party trick.'

'I reckon he'll tire, though. Let's keep up the pressure.' With that we were off in pursuit again – only to be thwarted by another duck-dive soon afterwards. Suffice to say, we tired long before he did and the laughing faces of a string of folk on the bank added to our embarrassment. To cap it all, someone had called the press and a reporter was waiting for us when we came ashore to consider our next course of action. Normally, Ged was patient with the press, but it seemed that his feathers had been ruffled after our antics in the boat and our failure to secure the bird.

'Hi, lads,' the reporter began, a grin spreading like a rash across his eager young face. Like policemen, reporters seem to get younger with the passing years.

'Put your cap on,' whispered Ged. 'Where there's a reporter there'll be a photographer somewhere.'

'Yes. Can I help you?' I enquired.

'Alan Bigley,' he announced, expecting us to know the name and distinctly cheesed off when we didn't.

'What rag are you from?' asked Ged, none too pleasantly.

'The local *Examiner*. You'll be a reader, I suppose.'

'Nah,' said Ged. 'When I want to read a comic I buy the *Beano*.' To his credit, the reporter took that one on the chin, but I was determined to deal with him myself from then on as I could see that Ged was heading for trouble out of sheer frustration. After a series of mocking questions as to why we hadn't caught the bird 'even with a boat available' and generally implying that we were total incompetents he asked when we'd be trying again. I told him the next afternoon about 2 p.m. The obnoxious Bigley departed and I tackled Ged.

'What's up with you, sore arse?'

'I haven't got a sore arse.'

'You will have after the chief's finished kicking it.'

He laughed. 'Aye. You're right, Steve. It's just you try your best and all parasites like him want to do is knock you and criticize.'

'They're not all like that in my admittedly limited experience.'

'Fair enough. But on days like these . . . That bird's really suffering and I, we, haven't put a stop to it. That hurts me – bloody hurts me it does!'

'Right. But, if you're up to it tomorrow, I've a Plan B.'

'Just give me a bell and I'll be over with the boat in a jiff.'

We arranged to meet at the lodge at 9.30 a.m. and I went home for tea.

Kathie greeted me with our little daughter in her arms. I took her into mine and smothered her with kisses. As usual, Kathie had spent the whole day on her own with Emma and, back then, I didn't appreciate how hard it was for her with no friends or relatives in the neighbourhood. I could see that she was tired out, though.

'I'll get something from the chippy,' I said. 'You're not up to cooking a meal.'

'Do I look that bad?'

172

'You know what I mean.'

'It's all right, Steve. There's some mince cooking. I'll add some herbs, onions and tomatoes and make an Italian – of sorts.'

'My mouth's watering already.' I turned to the little 'un. 'See, Em. Are you going to be a good cook like your mum and your grandmas?'

She gurgled, said 'Mama' and tried to push my nose through the back of my head – something quite a few of my clientele over the years might have been happy to attempt.

'By the way,' Kathie remembered. 'Headquarters have been on. You're to travel down to Horsham next week to have a roof rack fitted and bring back some ladders.'

'That's crazy. Why can't we buy them locally?'

'Better ask,' she replied. So I did. While Emma sat in her high chair vacuuming up her tea and watching a repeat episode of *Button Moon* starring one Mr Spoon I rang Horsham and spoke to one of the superintendents. He agreed with me but said it was a matter for Purchasing. I spoke to the head of Purchasing, who told me the Chief Officer Inspectorate had issued the instruction. Apparently, his mission was to centralize the collection of stores and equipment which, once achieved, would 'rationalize' the system, save time, and improve efficiency in the long run. Save time? It was a twelve-hour round trip for me. Nevertheless, I gave up and resigned myself to the journey, unnecessary as it was. I made a few more phone calls relating to the rescue of the duck and took my evening calls before settling down to a family cuddle on the settee.

The next morning Ged and I met at Hagg Lodge at 9.30 and prepared the boat. It wasn't long before we were joined by the Lancashire Police Frogman Unit from Preston who had agreed to help in the rescue as they had nothing urgent on and it could be classed as an excellent training exercise for them. All in a good cause, too. I had struck lucky with these guys, who wouldn't ordinarily have attended a job such as this and could easily have been busy assisting on a murder or some other serious crime investigation. They'd brought along their boat and, of course, a frogman, Ken Allsop.

'If we don't get him today, Ged, he's beaten us. Two boats, lots of bodies and a frogman in the water. Surely that's enough?'

'I've never managed to get these guys out,' he replied. 'Incredible. Well done, mate.'

We explained the situation to Ken and the others and it was decided to approach the bird from both sides in the boats, flanking the frogman who, hopefully, might be able to move in unnoticed. As we tried the tactic for the first time the duck dived as before. The frogman followed underwater and expectations were high, only to be crushed a little later when he emerged covered in weeds but empty handed. Daffy, as the press later called him, surfaced to starboard well away from our boats.

We regrouped in the middle of the lodge ready for another attempt. By now, quite a crowd had gathered on the bank to cheer us on. There was no doubt that the rescue was the hot ticket in town that day and news of

our endeavours to catch the stricken bird had spread
like wildfire. The numbers of folk on the bank swelled by
the minute.

Ken Allsop, the frogman, told us to keep our distance
in the boats and our nets lowered out of sight while he
tried a manoeuvre he had in mind. We idled along fifty
yards or so behind him and watched him disappear underwater again in front of us. The duck, seeing our boats so
far away, sensed no immediate danger and was barely
edging forward through the water when, suddenly, there
was an almighty splash and a whirl of foam surrounding
him. Ken the frogman emerged like a missile from below
and grabbed Daffy before he knew what was happening.
The bewildered bird struggled and put up a spirited fight
for freedom but the frogman held on and wasn't going to
let go. A tremendous cheer went up from the watching
crowd as we raced to reach him in the boats. He handed
over the startled duck and I gently but firmly lowered him
into a basket which I carefully secured. Ged and I thanked
the police team for attending and all their efforts on the
bird's behalf. Ken the frogman, the real hero of the rescue,
took some stick from his fellow officers when we were all
finally ashore.

'Here, Ken. You play cricket, don't you?'

'When I get a chance.'

'Bowler, aren't you?'

'That's right.'

'Not so great with the bat though?'

'No.'

'So it's not the first time you've been out for a duck then?'

'Bloody comedian!'

After another round of thanks to everyone concerned I set off for Halfords with the duck, as I thought it might need anaesthetising to remove the crossbow bolt from its wing. It was near to lunchtime already, when vets might be thin on the ground. When I arrived old Henry and his younger son, Morris, were out on a horse job at an isolated farm up Pickup Bank way but Barry, the elder son, was still on the premises and ushered me into a consulting room without delay. I thought he might have difficulty removing the bolt but it came out fairly easily with some careful manipulation. A close examination of the wing revealed three separate fractures and an infected wound swarming with maggots.

'It's a mess, Steve.'

'I can see.'

'It's not recent either. These maggots are a fair size. I'm sorry, but in my view it's the end of the road for him.'

There was no doubt in my mind that the vet was right and the humane option was to put the bird out of its misery, but I said, 'The funds are there if there's any hope at all.'

He paused, then shook his head. 'Money doesn't come into it. We'd do it for nothing as it's wildlife.' In one sense it seemed that all our efforts had been for nothing but, looking at it objectively, the bird wouldn't suffer any longer. Not the outcome we'd hoped for, but some small consolation all the same.

Pictures were taken and I made a point of contacting my local paper and giving them an exclusive on the rescue – in recognition of the work of the police underwater unit and their assistance in catching the bird. I pictured in my mind that intrepid newshound, Alan Bigley from the *Examiner*, arriving at Hagg Lodge that afternoon to find it deserted except for the odd fisherman and a few nesting ducks. Having missed all the action and excitement of the morning, he would sooner or later have to face an angry editor who wanted to know why.

# TWELVE

After a short acclimatization period and increasing hands-on experience in the job things were generally running smoothly in Lancs East and I was coping reasonably well with everything that was thrown at me. The only thing I really struggled with were phone calls late at night and, sometimes, in the early hours of the morning. I'm the sort that needs his sleep, a full eight hours plus, to function properly – not a good qualification, admittedly, for my chosen occupation. I didn't mind the genuine emergency calls – they came with the territory, so to speak. It was the calls that were not emergencies or in any way urgent and woke the whole household unnecessarily that rankled.

Some of the calls were laughable and, when I look back, almost surreal. A fine example was the disgruntled drunk I discovered on the end of the line at three o'clock one morning. 'Hello. Is that the animals?' He paused to burp and desperately catch his breath. It was difficult to restrain my mischievous streak just then. He had brought to mind

Eric Burdon and the famous sixties pop group the Animals and I very nearly replied 'It's the House of the Rising Sun', following up with 'I can recommend the crispy wontons and the black bean soup'. Before I had a chance, though, the voice warbled on. 'Hallo. It's me again. Are you there?'

'Yes. Can I help you?'

'If you're the animals . . .'

'Yes, it's the RSPCA. How can I help?'

'Well . . . it's like this . . .'

'Carry on.'

'It's like this . . .' Burp! 'I was on the way home – from the Shamrock in Brierley Street. I spotted this fair still on . . . dodgems an' all like. So I goes over and there's this hoopla stall. You know. You throw a hoop round somethin' and get a prize, eh?' I was running out of patience by then and, rather sharply, told him to get to the point.

'The flamin' point is this, inshpector . . . I won a blinkin' goldfish!' The Society's view was that goldfish should not be given as prizes by travelling fairs but in those days it was still common practice. I waited for him to continue. 'I don't know' – burp – 'what to do with it. I've never had a goldfish, have I? Can you eat 'em?'

'No,' I replied hurriedly. 'You'll have to get a book on their care from the library, or buy one, tomorrow . . . I mean today.'

'That's . . . that's all very well, my mate. But what about tonight?' I gave him advice on the welfare of goldfish but I doubted much of it was going in. Ideally, he'd need a tank and be prepared to equalize the temperature of the water in it with that of the water in the plastic bag before releasing the fish. Then, of course, he'd need food. No chance. I asked him where he was?

'Clitheroe . . . near the town centre church.'

'Wait there,' I told him. 'I'll be with you soon.'

I found the goldfish in its plastic bag near the church – hanging from one of the benches provided by a thoughtful rural district council. There was no sign of the caller, who'd probably wandered off, well oiled as he was, into the cloudy but balmy night.

The next day I took the goldfish to the animal shelter at Altham and Sylvia found an old glass tank and some recently donated fish food, both of which came in very handy in the circumstances. A shady spot in the office meant the inevitably named Goldie became a favourite with everybody, including the kennel girls who cleaned out and exercised the dogs every day. To avoid any confusion, only one of the girls was allowed to feed him, as accidental over-feeding could foul the water and lead to other problems. He also became a favourite with the shelter cat, which we had to keep an eye on.

I scrounged a cup of coffee, black with no sugar, at the shelter and took my time over it – much longer than usual. The late-night call had, predictably, got to me and I would have loved to linger in the comfortable office chair all afternoon, but Sylvia had just answered the phone and she turned in my direction. Putting her hand over the mouthpiece she whispered, 'I think this one's for you, Steve.' I took the phone from her and caught the words 'it's stuck'.

'Can I help?' I enquired.

'I hope so,' said the caller. He had one of those flat, monotone voices that drone on like a wasp trapped in a tumbler. 'There's a cat under a Rover car here with its head stuck. It's going nowhere at the moment.'

'Where are you?'

'Tythebarn Street, Darwen. Number forty-one. Pickles is the name – mine, not the cat's.'

'Give me quarter of an hour or so and I'll be with you,' I replied.

On the journey over to Darwen I was weighing up the situation I expected to face and wondering if I'd need the fire lads or even a mechanic to help release the unfortunate animal. Cats often rest under recently parked cars, enjoying the temporary warmth and relative security to be found there, and I knew of cases where they'd become trapped one way or another, including inside the engine compartment. Headquarters would have to be informed and foot the bill if necessary.

Arriving in Tythebarn Street, I quickly located a dark brown Rover and the concerned, monotone Mr Pickles. I looked under the car and was stunned by what I saw. Instead of being stuck under the vehicle itself the cat had its head actually stuck in an empty tin of Whiskas cat food. Obviously, I had got hold of the wrong end of the stick on the phone earlier. I decided to get my grasper from the van and, on the way, rethink the situation. By the time I got back to the car I had a Plan B. A passing cyclist was flagged down and offered to help and a chap standing in his doorway across the road was dragged over. With everyone present and correct, I felt like a CO addressing his troops as I explained what I intended to do.

'There's four escape routes the cat can take given its location,' I pointed out. 'Front, back or the driver and passenger sides. I want one of us covering each side.' Accompanying me as I spoke was the sound of intermittent barking from a back yard nearby.

'That's Otis,' explained Mr Pickles. 'Dean Shelley's dog. If the cat gets into his yard there'll be nothing much left to look at.' I gave Mr Pickles an expressive look.

'And let's keep it quiet,' I pleaded. 'He might be blind but he's not deaf. We don't want to spook him. If he starts heading for your side of the vehicle make a racket so he'll think twice. We've got to keep him under the car if we can. I've a better chance of collaring him there than anywhere else.'

As we approached, bending low, I kept an eagle eye on the black and white cat. The tin can looked to be firmly attached, covering his mouth, nose and jaw line right up to his ears. It must have been strange and frightening for him, unable to see all of a sudden. Probably, his struggles to free himself from his bizarre headgear had only pushed it on more securely. He looked like an owned animal but, frightened and disorientated by his predicament, he would almost certainly revert to his feral instincts when he became aware of our presence. A lot of folk are unaware just how quickly a domesticated cat can return to its fundamentally wild nature. It can be a matter of weeks rather than months. Yet to bring a feral cat round to domesticity is a painstaking and laborious task requiring endless patience and determination over a long period of time. Even then, the cat will only be truly at ease with those who have tamed it and will always remain wary of anyone else.

I tried not to make a noise with my grasper as I looked to position the rope round the cat's neck, but it clipped the side of the tin can. He panicked and ran but hit a rear tyre and came to a halt again.

'You've got him now, surely,' exclaimed Mr Pickles, in far too strident tones. The cat set off towards the passenger side of the car where the cyclist reacted quickly. He rang his bell and yelled, causing the cat to turn and run round in ever decreasing circles till, exhausted, it flopped to the ground. Taking my chance, I secured him with the grasper and gently pulled him slowly towards me. When he was clear of the car I managed to deposit him safely in a cat basket I'd brought along. I thanked everyone for their help and whisked the cat away (pardon the pun) to Halfords where Morris Halford interrupted some minor surgery on a Rottweiler to deal with us.

A veterinary nurse transferred the cat from my basket to the examination table and collected a few scratches on her arm for her trouble. The vet, with the nurse and myself holding the cat securely, managed to remove the tin can by gently twisting and turning it. Nevertheless, it took him a good few minutes to achieve his object. As the cat blinked in the bright lights of the surgery and realized

the world it used to know was still there the expression of
bewilderment and relief on its face was quite something to
see. I wished I'd had my camera at the ready to record the
moment for posterity. Morris gave him a shot of antibiotics
and I got him into the shelter the next day. It was a happy
ending for Whiskers, as I named him. His owner turned up
to claim him about ten days later. Luckily there were no
time limits at Altham then and an animal was in for as long
as it took to find a new home. I put up posters in Darwen
warning of the danger of discarded rubbish to pets and
wildlife – complete with pictures of Whiskers with head
stuck in the tin can.

Shortly after the cat and tin-can incident I had to collect
Region 7 North-West's roof rack and ladders from headquarters and deliver them to Manchester. I set off for Horsham
around 6 a.m. on a fine summer's morning. Kathie and I
had developed a keen interest in English parish churches,
both spiritually and in wonder at the ancient architecture. If
it worked out, I was determined to take my lunch break at
Middleton Cheney, where there was a church I particularly
wanted to see. If it lived up to expectations it would make
the whole nonsensical trip worthwhile.

It was well before midday when I parked the van near
All Saints church in the little Northamptonshire village
and found a seat in the churchyard to eat my ham salad
sandwiches, washed down with Kathie's excellent coffee.
It had kept remarkably warm in the old family flask I'd
inherited from my gran a few years back. The exterior of

the church itself, of red ironstone with spire and gargoyles, was impressive but it was the windows that I'd come to see.

Commissioned in the 1860s by the rector, William Buckley, they are fine examples of Morris, Burne-Jones and the rest of the Pre-Raphaelite brotherhood's work that Kathie had always loved. Eventually, I had come to admire their work myself, thanks to her passion and enthusiasm. I was reminded of Cohen again and his song 'Came So Far for Beauty', remembering, in fact, that I had.

Once inside All Saints I was not disappointed. I won't go into detail here, but if you're passing Middleton Cheney do yourself a favour and visit the church. Should it be locked as, sadly, so many are these days then raise Cain to get hold of a key or someone to let you in. If you get to see just a single window, let it be the magical west one by Burne-Jones . . . or, perhaps, Morris's east window in the south aisle. No . . . make sure you take time out to see them all and make it a real day to remember.

Reluctantly, I got back on the road to face the rest of the journey, which in those pre-M25 days meant driving through the likes of Slough and Staines. Further on was Leatherhead – which always reminded me of the weirdo in *The Texas Chain Saw Massacre*. By the early afternoon I was back in Horsham again at the reception desk at the manor house. Headquarters didn't seem to have changed much and the receptionist who couldn't get my name right when I came down for the interview was still there . . . and still couldn't get my name right.

'Inspector Greenhouse 226 . . . Are you sure that's right?'

'Only the 226 part. Just put me right for the Stores department, will you?'

Ten minutes later, having followed the receptionist's directions to the letter, I had to admit defeat. Yet again, I was lost in the old rabbit warren with no idea where I was. I knocked on the nearest door and an authoritative voice replied, 'Come in.' I prayed it wasn't the chief officer's hidey-hole. Anywhere but that. I might not have been able to resist offering him my views on 'centralization' and walking out with my P45 in my hand.

'Ah, Mr Daltrey, is it?' enquired the small rotund man in a smart blue suit parked behind a large desk. He rose to greet me and offered to shake my hand.

'Er . . .'

'From Cock-up Computers . . . very droll, that. Sit down, please.'

I declined his outstretched hand and remained standing. 'I'm not Mr Daltrey, I'm afraid.'

'Oh. Is the poor chap ill? Have you come in his place?'

'No. I'm not from Cock-up Computers at all.'

He looked deflated and puzzled. 'Well, who the blazes are you, then?'

'I was wondering the same thing.'

'Wondering who you are?'

'Who you are, actually.'

'Sinton-Davies. Overseas department.'

'Inspector Greenhalgh, 226, Lancashire East branch.'

We looked each other over suspiciously. I was half expecting him to order me out but he began to laugh – like a drain, in fact.

'It's a cock-up then but not of the computer kind,' he said, regaining his composure. We chatted amicably over a cup of tea and he was only too happy to put me right for the Stores department. He even offered me a pinch of snuff as I was leaving. To be honest, I rather liked Sinton-Davies. He might have looked like the worst kind of stuffy, stuck-up southerner but, in every way, he was a larger than life character with a fine sense of humour. I did wonder though at the concept of an overseas department. Why go looking for problems abroad when there are so many here? I suppose he'd have called me a 'little Englander' with no breadth of vision, but I think he would have said it with conviction and humour, which I admire. As I continued on my weary way to the Stores department I rounded a corner and collided with a man hurrying in the opposite direction.

'Sorry.'

'Yes. Sorry,' he echoed. Having exchanged regrets for interrupting each other's progress recognition gradually dawned.

'Doc! It's you, isn't it?' I was sure it was the medicine man who had condemned me to a lifetime of glasses and regular eye tests.

'Oh, you! Greengage, isn't it?'

'Something like that,' I agreed.

'Glad to see you've got some glasses at last.'

'Thanks to you.'

'You really shouldn't have been driving that day, you know.' I hadn't the heart to tell him I'd driven back home as well – of necessity. Anyway, he was on his way again in a flash and soon afterwards I found the Stores department in its remote, secluded spot.

'Greenhalgh, 226,' I announced to the tall, lean chap in a brown overall who ran the show. He looked round slowly and I immediately noticed the likeness to Smiler in *Last of the Summer Wine* – hangdog face, drooping moustache and world-weary aspect.

'Roof rack and ladders for region 7?' he asked.

'Spot on, is that. You must be psychic.'

'Not really. You're the only one left on today's list except for locals.' Together, we fitted the roof rack and carefully secured the ladders. My van suddenly took on the appearance of a mobile, medieval battering ram or, stretching the imagination even further, a huge metallic bird of prey.

'Word of warning,' said the man from Stores.

'Yes?'

'Take it easy on the motorway on your way back. That lot will slow you down anyway, but . . . there's been incidents.'

'Incidents?'

'Incidents that almost became accidents.'

I looked surprised and suitably impressed. 'What sort of incidents that almost became accidents?' I asked. His moustache twitched and a sharp intake of breath followed.

'Suffice to say, things can work loose and a nod's as good as a wink.'

'Can they? Is it?' Before I could question him further on the subject of nods and winks or even roof racks and ladders he produced a chitty. After several bad experiences in the past, I confess, I have never grown fond of chitties but it was clear that they were meat and drink to the man in the brown overall.

'Sign here,' he demanded. 'It's a chitty to confirm you've received the said items.'

I examined the official-looking document closely. 'But I haven't.'

'Course you have!' he exclaimed loudly. 'What do you think they are?' He pointed to the roof rack and ladders on my van.

'A roof rack and ladders.'

'Well . . . sign the chitty then.'

'But this chitty's for a swan hook and waders.'

He grabbed it back as if a mistake couldn't possibly have happened. Then his face fell.

'Ah! That's Inspector Farley, 101, arriving 4 p.m. Blimey!' He reached deep into the two front pockets of the long brown overall but, disappointingly, the missing chitty failed to emerge from either. 'I must have left it on my desk. I'll not be a couple of minutes.'

After fifteen of them, he hadn't returned and I set off on the long journey home. Being delayed by storm and tempest, snow or heavy traffic was one thing – or four, possibly – but I refused to be held up a minute longer by a missing chitty. Mind you, I did take the man in the brown overall's advice and keep my speed down on the motorway. In fact, driving was distinctly unpleasant with the addition of the 'said items' above me that I hadn't signed for. Nevertheless, thoughts of Morris and Co's glass and returning home to Kathie and Emma spurred me on and I finally arrived on our drive around 8 p.m.

The following morning I delivered the roof rack and ladders to my chief inspector in Manchester, Des Pratt, who stored them in his garage in Worsley. They just about left room for one vehicle. Des, newly appointed and on improved chief inspector's pay, had a red sports car of his own as well as the Society's van. No prizes for guessing which of them saw the inside of the garage on a regular basis. As Des was about to close the doors I noticed a small metal plate attached to the side of one of the ladders.

'Hang on, chief.'

'What?'

'Let's have a butcher's at that plate on the ladders.'

'It's just info about the makers.'

'Exactly. I was wondering who they are.' I leaned forward to read the details on the plate . . .

Scrayingham & Co.
Chatburn Road
CLITHEROE
Lancs.

'I knew it!' I exclaimed.

'What's that?'

'I've just travelled five hundred miles or more to collect

ladders made by a firm ten miles from our house. And, of course, we'd have had to pay for them being delivered to headquarters beforehand. It's insane.'

'Welcome to the RS,' said Des, a huge grin illuminating his face.

One evening Kathie and I were looking through an album of old photographs, cringing at the toe-curling awfulness of some of them and enjoying others.

'You've put on a bit of weight since that holiday in the Lakes,' she insisted.

'Never. I've been the same weight for years now. Besides, look at you in Scotland.'

'What's wrong with me?' she demanded.

'Nothing's wrong. I'm just wondering where that princess went.'

'Same place as her prince, I should think.'

That's the trouble with old photographs. They tend to lead to disputes and disappointment. Where was such and such taken and what year? Was it just a bad hair day or, inexplicably, did you think you looked good like that? For instance, there are some people, men and women, who should never have a perm. Folk sporting ugly perms should be hauled off the streets and placed under curfew while they are instructed in the ways of social compatibility and good taste. A mullet should have remained solely a fish.

'Look at you smoking that daft pipe in this one.' Kathie was laughing. Before I could reply there was a sharp rap on the front door. We looked at each other in surprise as it was gone 11 p.m. People did call at the house intermittently, as it was known to be 'the RSPCA place'. The fact that it was also our home was neither here nor there to some folk, but I didn't mind if there was an injured or sick animal involved. It was only to be expected.

'It's bound to be for you,' said Kathie. I knew that she was right, of course, and went to answer the door. On the doorstep was a big fellow with a shaved head and tattoos down his arms, one of which featured the legend 'Man City Rule' with likenesses of three City stars – Bell, Summerbee and Lee – etched in below. He was a bit of a shock as an unexpected late-night caller, but despite appearances he came over as friendly and lucid.

'Sorry to call at this hour, mate. Are you the RSPCA man?'

'That's right.'

'I was over Blackpool way with the girlfriend today and on the beach we came across a seal pup. He looked ill – lethargic like. We didn't know what to do so we threw a blanket over him and brought him to the animal shelter here. We live close by.'

'It was closed, I suppose.'

'Spot on,' he replied. 'So we brought him here in the van. If you can't help I don't know what we'll do with him.'

'Let's have a look,' I said.

I put my coat on and joined him at the van. In the passenger seat a red-headed lass waved to us but carried on painting her face in the mirror. The City fan opened the rear doors cautiously and we peered inside. A pale, faltering light illuminated a young grey seal pup sitting on a blanket looking surprised and not particularly pleased to see us. I hopped in the back of the vehicle and asked the owner to shut the doors behind me.

The youngster tried to shuffle away from me but I managed to secure him without too much trouble. On examination, his breathing was laboured but he seemed to be in fair bodily condition. I picked him up in the blanket and kicked the doors of the van. They were opened wide and I jumped down.

'You got him safe, mate?'

'Safe and secure. Don't worry,' I replied.

'What will happen to him?'

'I'll take him in and get a vet to check him over. We'll see where we go from there.'

'Thanks . . . that's brilliant! I'll give you a bell tomorrow to see how he's gone on.'

'Fine.'

Inside the house, Kathie had guessed what I'd do and was clearing the bathroom in anticipation. I carried our late-night visitor upstairs in my arms and he was no trouble. They can give you quite a nip but he seemed to accept his fate without protest. Probably anything was better than the back of the Transit van.

'It's all right,' said Kathie, 'the bathroom's clear now.'

'How did you know?'

'I know you.'

I placed the pup gently in the bath and he looked up at us

in such an endearing, heartbreaking way that you couldn't help but fall for him. Nevertheless, as he flapped around helplessly we could clearly detect his breathing problem.

'I'm calling a vet,' I told Kathie.

'It's late, isn't it?'

'Can't be helped. I'll try Powell's. They're the nearest.'

Ronnie Powell sounded tired and grumpy when he answered my call. It wasn't unreasonable – it was approaching midnight and he'd had a hectic day at the surgery. His mood changed rapidly, though, when I told him about the seal pup – not something a vet sees every day.

'I'll be round inside half an hour,' he promised.

Ronnie was as good as his word and when he arrived he confirmed that the pup had a respiratory problem. Then came the awkward bit.

'Hold him tight, Steve. He's not going to like this.' Ronnie moved into position and proceeded to take the pup's rectal temperature. If such a cute creature can be said to give someone a dirty look I reckon Ronnie got one then. I could just imagine the pup thinking, 'These humans. They don't half have some strange rituals and ideas. Bonkers, really.' After all, how was he to know it was for his own good?

The vet decided to take the seal pup with him to his surgery where he could be treated further and monitored overnight by the veterinary nurse who lived on the premises. We were sad to see him go, but of course it was for the best. As the pup lay wrapped in the blanket in the back of the vet's Volvo he lifted his head for one final time to look at us and we bent forward and stroked him. That was it. We never saw the little fellow again.

After a short period of treatment, recovery and specialist care I was told that the pup had been released at a suitable location on the coast. Kathie and I often think about that extraordinary night when, just for a while, we had a seal pup in the bath.

# THIRTEEN

I was busy clipping the front hedge with Dad's old shears one day when the phone rang. I'd left the door open so I could hear it as Kathie was out shopping. It was Ged in Bolton. The moment I put the phone down after his call Jeff Knowles was on from Bury. The subject was the same – compulsory redundancies.

Apparently, the RSPCA was unexpectedly in deep financial trouble and, to get back on an even keel, there would have to be a reduction in inspector numbers. It would be on a last-in first-out basis, according to the rumours flying about, which meant I was under serious threat of losing the job I loved and the roof over our heads. In a state of shock, I told Kathie later that evening when our daughter was fast asleep. There were no tears – just a hug for me.

'What shall we do then?' she whispered. For the time being I had no answer and replied with a sigh and a shrug of my shoulders.

A meeting of the Society's inspectors throughout the country was arranged by management within a few weeks of the calls from Ged and Jeff Knowles. Headquarters were well aware of the rumour mill and wanted to explain the situation and how they planned to deal with it. There were plenty of worried faces that day in the big hall in Birmingham where the meeting was held. I met Marvin again for the first time since we'd been trainees and it was good to see him once more despite the circumstances.

'Rescued any kittens up trees lately?' he asked.

'Still supping the Bolli on our wages? I replied. 'Is this as far north as you've ever been, Marvin?'

'As far as I ever want to.' We had a drink together during the lunch break and he told me he was transferring to the SIU, the Special Investigations Unit, in a few months time. This had been set up as a task force with issues like the export of live food animals, dog and cock fighting and badger baiting in mind. It often involved trips abroad and periods away from the family – something I would never have contemplated but which Marvin seemed happy with.

'Billingshurst will be glad to see the back of you,' I joked.

'How's Accrington then? Have you got a toilet inside your house yet or are you still havin' to leg it down the back yard?' The banter continued till it was time to hear the bad news from the top table. Basically, there would have to be cutbacks and, yes, redundancies within the Inspectorate but 'every effort will be made to keep the losses voluntary rather than compulsory'. For a few inspectors in their mid-fifties and sixties the packages offered to retire early were quite attractive, though even so how anyone would want to give up the job was incomprehensible to me and I went away still expecting the worst. It had been made clear that any compulsory redundancies would indeed be on the dreaded last-in first-out basis.

As the meeting ended Marvin and I shook hands and wished each other well. I told him to pop in on us if his enquiries and investigations ever led him north of Brum up Manchester way to civilization, not to mention people who really were the salt of the earth. He laughed and, as he waved goodbye, shook his head. The last I heard from him was, 'Keep burning the witches!'

When I got home that night I skipped tea and stayed up late staring into the fire in the darkness with a can of lager for company. Dad had recently died or, late as it was, I'd have probably rung him at home for reassurance and advice. Why does nobody leave a phone number when they die? Like most sons, I'd been much closer to my mother as a child, but it sort of reversed after adolescence. Whenever I visited home I expected to see him in his old armchair, a gardening or fishing book close to hand. Keeping the garden in good shape was impossible for Mum or myself though I regularly mowed the back lawn – thinking all the time how much better it had looked when Dad had done it. It's said that you can't go back and that's right, but sometimes, what we'd all give if we could. Just before I slipped into a deep melancholy, Marvin came back to mind and his 'keep burning the witches' remark brought a smile to my face. I got up from the sofa and put my headphones on before selecting a record. Soon after, Hendrix drenched my ears with sound and a little bit of 'Spanish Castle Magic' washed away the world, at least till the next morning.

The RSPCA is an admirable organization that performs many wonders, though not necessarily intentionally. The morning after the trip to Birmingham and my late night the post arrived about 7 a.m. as always. Feeling tired, fed up and irritable I collected the letters and looked through them over a light breakfast of toast and coffee. Not unexpectedly, there was one from headquarters in the usual plain brown envelope with a Horsham postmark.

As a rule, the contents of headquarters envelopes are pertinent and instructive but by no means a barrel of laughs, so, feeling the way I did, I opened this one with no great enthusiasm. I should have known better. Trust my elders and betters to cheer me up and bring forth a smile where once there'd been a frown, foster well-being despite lingering uncertainty, and induce wonder at such pettifogging inanity and blather. Amongst the usual case instructions, circulars and information sheets was a 'Compilation List of All Approved and Non-Approved Items'. Apparently, a small, high-powered group of mugs acting on their own absurd instincts had thought long and hard about the items an inspector should have in his possession and be allowed to carry in the Society's van. Why such an exercise was strictly necessary in the first place is open to question, but some of the dimmest intellects in the Inspectorate and elsewhere must have been huddled together in a dark room to come up with the list I was now browsing through in a state of increasing amusement and bewilderment.

It seems that I could have a hammer but not an axe. So, something carried by the infamous Yorkshire Ripper was okay but a lumberjack's implement was a no-no. I could have wire cutters and bolt croppers but on no account possess traffic cones or a tyre inflator. Functional mittens (but only HQ issue) were perfectly acceptable but Lord help the inspector caught with a towing rope or jump leads which might actually have proved useful. Incidentally, who would want non-functional mittens? Disposable shoe covers were a must, of course, but a life-saving fire extinguisher was out of the question. Also given the red-light treatment were small ladders (for looking over walls). The explanatory information in brackets as to the use of small ladders gives you some idea of the compilers' opinion of the everyday inspector's intellectual ability. Then there were gardening gloves – strictly not approved. Perhaps they were afraid a branch secretary might cajole an inspector into pruning her roses after their weekly meetings, resulting in a serious neglect of duty. Finally, and my all-time favourite banned item (though it was a close thing), the British Rail fluorescent vest. For certain, the average inspector wouldn't have had access to nor gone out of their way to obtain a railwayman's fluorescent vest. But pity the few who had and now found them on the non-approved items list.

The sort of witless, bureaucratic thinking involved in the compilation of such a document is hard to comprehend but not uncommon in large organizations. The RSPCA, as I increasingly discovered, was far from immune from such nonsense. In fact there were times when it felt as if you were marooned in a Monty Python sketch with John Cleese running the show as chief officer and Eric Idle as your chief inspector. Probably, a committee had been formed at headquarters at the time to consider the approval or non-approval of the dead parrot sketch. It sounds absolutely crazy but it is *just* possible such a thing actually happened. After all, a camel is a horse designed by a committee.

Despite the draconian list of non-approved items I reckon almost every serving inspector was in breach of it. I admit to the possession and transportation of a non-approved goldfish net and a horse blanket. Ged, I know, once showed me an illegal amber flashing beacon he claimed to use quite frequently in the rush to get to emergencies. There was also a shifty fellow I knew who, to spare inevitable embarrassment, shall remain nameless. He secreted udder wipes – specifically non approved – in his vehicle, confident no one would ever find them there. The rascal!

I remember that I was stopped a couple of times for speeding and on both occasions I was on my way to urgent calls, an injured cat and another, rather different, job. Of course, I was out of order twice over and I make no excuses. I collected the points on my licence and made sure I drove within the limit afterwards – much to the annoyance it has to be said of many of my fellow motorists. I couldn't allow their frustration to influence me. My ability to drive was essential to performing my duties as an inspector and losing my licence would have had the same effect as being made redundant. I'm quite proud of the fact that, despite driving three to four hundred miles a week for the best part of three decades, the two speeding fines and, much later, one for allegedly running a red light whilst on duty in Preston were all the traffic offences I accumulated during my career with the Society. Oh, and one parking fine in Accrington.

Going back to the call that led to my second speeding offence: it was New Year's Eve and the country was in the grip of some seriously wintry conditions. Snow had fallen during the last week and I'd taken a few days' leave. Kathie and I had been up to Oak Hill Park and gone sledging with Emma. The snow-covered slope from the trees at the top near the war memorial to the bottom path near Manchester Road was steep. The snow had tempted plenty of families outdoors that day and the view across the road over the white, sun-dappled fields to the coppice was pretty spectacular. As we waited our turn to tackle the slope our breath froze in the air. Both my girls looked cute in their bright scarves, bobble hats and wellingtons and Kathie and I took turns on the sledge holding Emma. It was an exhilarating experience that I'll never forget. Once, we even crossed the path at the bottom and, fortunately, fell off the sledge before we hit some thick bushes near the wall. The day stands out so clearly in my mind because there have been so few snowy winters since. In my own childhood snow was almost guaranteed at some time during winter and, yes, even occasionally fell at Christmas.

The job itself came in during my lunchtime calls and, to be honest, my heart sank. Some residents of a large block of flats, an eyesore on the local landscape in Blackburn, had found a snake on one of the walkways and had managed to secure the reptile in a budgie cage they'd scrounged off someone in a neighbouring flat. Naturally enough, they wanted it collected as soon as possible.

The reason my heart sank was simple – I didn't exactly like snakes. It wasn't the classic phobia. I'd inspected local pet shops that stocked them and discussed their welfare with the proprietors next to tanks containing them. Nevertheless, they weren't on my favourites list and, at the time, I hadn't handled one (something I corrected later and which changed my outlook and thinking on reptiles in general). Back then, Ged or Jeff Knowles could usually be relied on to help out if a snake job turned up but they were both on leave, I discovered, so there was nothing for it but to face my demons and crack on. Before I set off I rang the shelter on the off chance they'd take the snake.

'Sylvia. It's Steve.' I heard the sigh at the other end of the line.

'I guessed that one.'

'Now, don't be like that. Who sorts out all your problems, drives you to branch meetings and sticks up for you against Miss Potts, Mrs Hall and the rest?'

'I don't know, but if you see them give them my thanks.'

'I was wondering . . .'

'Sorry.'

'For what?'

'To disappoint you. We're really at bursting point here, Steve.'

'It wouldn't take up much room, I'm sure.'

'What wouldn't?'

'The snake. Once I've had him identified, of course.'

'You bring a snake up here, Steve Greenhalgh, and I'll arrange for someone to wrap it round your neck and strangle you with it!'

'Not your cup of tea then?'

'Not really,' she agreed. 'But, regardless, we've simply no facilities anyway. Try those vets in Blackpool. They're into herp . . . herp . . .'

'Herpes?'

'Herpawhatsitology.' Clearly, I had to forget about the shelter on this occasion. Finding the number of the vets Sylvia had mentioned was a problem in as much as I couldn't bring to mind the name of the practice. Then, suddenly, it clicked – Hatton and Ripslinger – that was it. Much to my relief, they were happy to examine the reptile and admit it for a few days. So far, so good. I hoped the vet on duty would be Ripslinger so I could ask him about his extraordinary name.

By then, I'd been a lot longer on the phone than I'd intended and I felt I needed to make up for lost time. This in turn led me to step on the gas and I was doing 37 in a 30 mph zone when a traffic policeman flagged me down. He must have had an excellent hidey-hole as I hadn't noticed him till the last minute. I knew that however diplomatic I tried to be, and however worthy my cause, it would count for nothing. In those days, traffic officers were real hardliners. They wouldn't let fireworks off on bonfire night. This one even lectured me at length on the subject of more haste less speed as he handed me my ticket. I asked him if he'd like to be the proud owner of the snake I was going to collect should it remain unclaimed.

'The place for snakes is in the grass!' he proclaimed, ridiculously. Leaving Proverb Man laughing as he filled in his notebook, I resumed my journey – at a rather slower pace.

I arrived, very late, at the block of flats and went in search of Westminster Court amongst all the other courts detailed on a rectangular metal plate screwed to the wall at an entrance point. The place was a graffiti-ridden testament to those smug, self-satisfied, ineffably stupid sixties architects who condemned huge chunks of the population to live in identical prison cells in the sky. Places where children couldn't play out and the stairs and walkways were little more than corridors of crime. How Britain sleepwalked into tower-block trauma and demolished its stock of, in many cases, perfectly good terraced housing is a mystery. All they needed was refurbishment . . . all they got was the wrecking ball. The country, or rather those in charge of it, seem to enjoy such self-inflicted wounds and there have been many more since the sixties.

As I approached the door of number 23 Westminster Court I paused and took a deep breath. A youngster answered the door and led me through to the living room. Sure enough, there was a budgie cage on the dining table and coiled up inside was the snake. It was over a metre long, quite slender, with orangey-brown skin and regular darker-coloured bands along its length. Mind, when it came to identification, it could have been pink and blue with stars and stripes as far as I was concerned. You can't be an expert or even knowledgeable about everything, though I've known some inspectors who resort to flannel and bluster when they're asked something and they don't know the answer. Ultimately, it just makes them look foolish. Far better to admit that you don't know, promise to find out and get back to whoever asked the question.

The fact is I had no idea whether the snake was venomous or harmless but one thing was obvious – it was angry. One bad-tempered reptile, for sure. As I went a bit nearer for a closer look it reared and struck repeatedly against the bars of the fragile budgie cage. I asked the people who had found it if it had been like this all the time and, if so, how the dickens they had caught it and put it in the cage.

'It was sleepy when we found it outside,' piped up the youngster. Clearly, the winter temperatures had kept the cold-blooded snake relatively docile, enabling the finders to secure it in the borrowed budgie cage. Once inside the flat it had slowly warmed up and come to life again. It seemed, also, to have remembered an old grudge and was out for revenge. It was then that I noticed that the door of the budgie cage was only secured by means of the handle of a teaspoon jammed into it. That was when the hairs on the back of my neck really started to tingle and I cursed my heartless colleagues enjoying their time off.

Transferring the snake into a more suitable container in such circumstances was impossible, or at least I deemed it so, particularly as I didn't know whether the creature was poisonous or not. I went back to the van and thought about things for a minute before deciding on a plan of action. Then I went back to the flat carrying a few things with me. I put on my clumsy, well-padded animal-handling gloves which would protect me from a bite or at least mitigate the effects of one. He didn't look like a spitter but, just in case, I wore goggles as I nervously approached the cage on the table. As before, I was watched with the utmost suspicion by the snake and, as before, he struck repeatedly at the bars near the dodgy door and the rattling handle of the teaspoon securing it. The comments from the family came thick and fast as I picked up the cage and held it at arm's length.

'Rather you than me, mate.'

'Don't drop it, for Gawd's sake!'

'Not in here anyway.'

'Blimey! Look at it havin' a go tryin' to get him.'

'You've got the wrong deodorant on, I reckon.'

'Take it easy till you're outside, eh?'

Out on the walkway I placed the budgie cage with its irate occupant in a cat basket and just about managed to close it. I then put the cat basket into a large cardboard box punctured with small air holes. The box was secured with tape and string. Finally, I put the box in a dog cage I'd had made recently by one of the voluntary branch workers who was a bit handy and wanted to help out. There were no 'sky kennels' issued by headquarters in those days, just dog guards to act as a barrier in the vehicles.

I was ill at ease when I set off for the vets in Blackpool. Despite the layers between us I couldn't rest easily and all the way, some twenty miles or more, I was regularly glancing in the mirror or over my shoulder to check that the snake wasn't loose and everything was all right. It was the most torturous and, because of my inattentive driving, dangerous journey I've ever undertaken.

Eventually, I reached Hatton and Ripslinger's surgery and took the cardboard box containing cat basket and budgie cage into one of their consultation rooms. I wanted to stay for the outcome of the examination but the branch secretary, who knew I'd be calling at the Blackpool surgery that afternoon, had phoned about an injured owl at a school in Blackburn. I said I'd ring the vets later and thanked them before retracing my tyre tracks to Blackburn. When I reached the school I examined the tawny owl and everything seemed fine. No apparent injuries suggested he had simply been stunned after hitting a window and I released him in a nearby field. He was flying perfectly normally as he disappeared over the horizon. After a few more jobs I reached home in good time for my evening calls and rang the vets in Blackpool. I hoped it would be Ripslinger rather than Hatton on the other end of the line. In the event, it was Sam Adams, a junior partner in the practice.

'Inspector Greenhalgh,' I said. 'I'm calling about the snake I left with you earlier today.'

'Ah, yes. We dug him out of your containers and

managed to get a good look at him. He's a corn snake. Not venomous but they can give you a nasty nip and, initially, this chap would have liked nothing better. It was clear that something was wrong as they're usually reluctant to bite and fairly docile.'

'So it wasn't just me he took a dislike to?'

'No, not at all. As a matter of interest, where was the snake found – near a heat source of any kind?'

'Not that I know of.'

'Hm,' said the vet. 'He's an area of skin that's been burned, which would account for the bad temper exhibited.'

'Can he stay with you for a few days? There's a possibility someone might claim him.'

'No problem. We can find suitable long-term lodgings if you're stuck.'

'Excellent. Thanks again for all your help,' I said. 'Oh – happy New Year, too.'

I was on duty that evening but it was deadly quiet and I celebrated the New Year with an orange juice and tonic water with Kathie before we went to bed. Through a gap in the curtains I could see a few stars shining in the dark velvet sky. I think they were my lucky ones and I thanked them for seeing me through another crazy day in a job that kept challenging me in so many different, unexpected ways, but I loved all the same.

# FOURTEEN

I received all sorts of complaints regarding cruelty to animals on a daily basis. Probably, on average, five or six a day. That doesn't seem like a lot but investigating them thoroughly, often miles apart, was more than one day's work. There was no doubt that Lancs East was a busy branch. In all honesty, though, I liked it like that, at least until the days when complaint overkill made it obvious that a second inspector was urgently needed in the area. Nevertheless, some complaints I received had a touch of humour about them that added greatly to the joys of existence. There was the one about a thin donkey at Knuzden near Blackburn from PC Bray. Then the one about a blind horse kept in a shed with no windows. I suppose the most bizarre and outrageous of them was the one about the goat. Oddly, it wasn't really a complaint about the animal itself, rather the goat's location and what it was doing. It fell to me, however, as the RSPCA inspector in the area to deal with the matter and, as the caller rather histrionically put it, deal with it 'reet sharpish'.

The call came from a keen-eyed member of the public who had been passing by the location and was amazed at what he saw. There on the Crown Ground, home of one of the most famous football teams in the land, Accrington Stanley, was a goat, standing in the middle of the pitch grazing nonchalantly on the sacred Stanley turf. The caller was almost brimming over with indignation and, as a football man myself, I could see why. He emphasized the quite seismic importance of the matter.

Stanley had gone bust mid-season in 1962, long before that sort of thing became fashionable. They had re-formed six years later and embarked on the long climb up the football pyramid with the ultimate aim of becoming a league club again. At the time of the goat's appearance the club's climb back to glory was in its infancy and the pitch not quite up to Old Trafford, Anfield or even Cheshire League first division standards. Still, a goat grazing on it and the effects of rain and mud was a recipe for disaster.

When I arrived at the club there was no one to be seen. Even the groundsman had finished for the day. I wondered how the goat had got in until I found a gap in the wooden fencing surrounding the pitch caused by vandals. I removed a few more boards and ducked through the opening I'd made. The goat, meanwhile, carried on regardless. I shouted repeatedly to see if anyone was around and eventually three men appeared, apparently from nowhere. One was the club chairman and the other two were officials of the Cheshire League who were there to assess ground improvements.

'Oh, the RSPCA. You're here at last,' yapped the relieved chairman. He was red faced with embarrassment at the goat's presence on the pitch while the ground was being inspected by VIPs. 'Can you remove that animal, please?'

'He's trespassing,' joked one of the officials.

'I thought he was the club's new lawnmower,' the other chimed in. The Stanley chairman faked a smile and gritted his teeth. He looked at me pleadingly and decided a sweetener might help.

'I've a free pair of tickets for the next home match. They're yours if you get on with the job.' He pushed them into my hand before I knew what was happening and led the two grinning League officials away.

Now, strictly, I wasn't allowed to accept gratuities but I wondered if football tickets might be an exception. After all, rightly or wrongly, I had already accepted a frozen chicken dumped on the passenger seat of my van by the grateful manager of a packing factory after catching an owl that was trapped in the place. I was told later that it was a grey area but, as a rule, it was better not to do so. I can honestly say that I never accepted anything again and I don't regret it – though the fresh goat's cheese on offer from a farmer's wife in Ribchester did tempt me something shocking.

I strolled up close to the intruder, a brown goat with flashes of white round its mouth, on its flanks and on all four legs. It turned out to be a castrated male (or wether) and I decided to ring Ged in Bolton who, I knew, had a covered trailer that would come in handy for transporting the animal. He arrived in no time carrying a few tasty food items. The goat proved quite cooperative and within ten minutes or so we had him enclosed in the trailer. He was in good condition and obviously a pet.

There were some pens about two hundred metres away at the bottom of Livingstone Road and we drove down there with a view to making enquiries. A man on one of the pens was making a cuppa in his shed and told us that a chap who lived on Stanley Street rented the nearby pen where the goat was usually kept. He didn't know the number of the house but it was the third one down from the top on the Burnley Road side of the street.

While we were there we checked out our friend's home and found he was well provided for. The pen was grassed and well drained, and there was fresh water present in an old bath. A handsome new shed full of clean, dry bedding material stood in one corner of the enclosure. Unlike sheep, goats don't have a waterproof coat and detest getting wet. They will try to find shelter whenever it rains and, in this case, there was no problem on that score. Thanking Ged for his invaluable assistance, I led the way in my vehicle to Stanley Street and the house in question.

We knocked hard on the front door. It was answered by a large man wearing dark trousers with red braces and dark blue slippers with yellow Noddy figures printed on them. By his side was a youngster, about twelve years of age, wearing similar, if smaller, Noddy slippers and an excited expression on his face as he took in our uniforms and wondered 'what were up'. I was first to speak.

'Hello. Inspector Greenhalgh and Inspector Hardwick, RSPCA,' I began. 'We're trying to trace the owner of a brown and white goat off a pen on Livingstone Road.'

The large man's pasty face fell. 'Nay! He's not gone and done a Houdini again, has he? I've put six-foot-high fences up, too. Come on in, lads . . . Dost want a brew?' Usually we didn't accept cups of tea and such but we were both ready for one that day so, on this occasion, we did. Ged and I followed the man and his son into the living room and sat down on the large sofa while they went off to make the tea. They returned a few minutes later and we gratefully accepted our cuppas.

'I hope there's enough milk in, lads,' said the father. Then, noticing the door wide open, he spoke to the boy. 'Hey, Stanley, lad. Put wood i' th' 'ole. We're freezin' in here.'

'Oh, Dad.'

'Get on wi' it or there'll be no tater 'ash for thee come teatime. You'll be skrikin' then, eh?'

I explained what had happened and asked him his name.

'Stanley,' he replied.

'And your son here's Stanley too?'

'Aye. Stanley junior.'

'And you live here – on Stanley Street?' asked Ged, barely believing what he was hearing.

'That's right,' said Stanley junior.

'What's the goat called?' I asked, already anticipating the answer.

'Stanley,' said the father, 'but sometimes we call him

Houdini seein' he's escaped that often.' Ged and I were trying not to laugh, and failing.

'Everybody laughs,' said the father.

'One more question,' said Ged. 'What's your favourite football team?'

'Burnley,' he replied. 'But we sometimes go on at Stanley if Burnley are away.'

We returned the goat to the pen, pointed out where the fence needed repairing and left father and son there. 'No one would credit it, would they?' I remarked.

'And, unbelievably,' said Ged, 'his surname's Kidd.'

When I got home there was a letter from headquarters waiting for me. I knew the decision on redundancies was due soon so I was apprehensive about opening it. One of the information sheets was headed 'Inspectorate Redundancies'. This was it, then. The magic words were in the final paragraph. 'Most of the necessary redundancies were achieved voluntarily. The few that weren't have been successfully negotiated and the matter is now closed.' A huge wave of relief blanketed my thoughts temporarily. Then, in a state of near euphoria, I set off in search of Kathie to tell her the good news.

A short while after the affair of the Stanleys and the good news on redundancies I collected a stray cat from an address in Simonstone, near Burnley. Jet black, four or five months old and as cute as anything on the planet, the young male was a prime candidate for rehoming. How anyone could abandon him was a mystery, but no one came forward to claim him. I got him in at the shelter and was about to leave when Sylvia's voice brought me to a halt. 'Inspector Greenhalgh,' she yelled, from behind me. I knew that if it wasn't Steve I was for it. 'Sit yourself down in that office and do the paperwork. You're always escaping and leaving it to us. Well, this time you're Johnny on the spot!'

I turned, laughed and held my hands up. 'Guilty,' I pleaded. 'It's a fair cop.' I headed for the office sharpish under Sylvia's watchful eye and began to fill in the boarding form. Now, in the case of strays or animals whose names weren't known one had to be supplied by the person filling in the form. In an attempt to avoid using the same old ones again and again I had become notorious for conjuring up dodgy monikers for the animals I brought to the shelter. Some, like Milverton, Mycroft, Musgrave and Moriarty, stemmed from my absorbing interest in the Sherlock Holmes stories. Others were connected with churches I'd visited at one time or another . . . Castor, Willoughby, Dunster and Barkwell – one of my best. There were some originating from Lanky dialect that seemed appropriate . . . Cratchy for a rather ill-tempered canine, Kecks for a ferret with a liking for running up trousers and Nobbut – meaning 'no more than' – for a slip of a pup who was the runt of a litter that had been abandoned on my doorstep by someone during the night.

Understandably, when the bizarrely named animals were rehomed by Sylvia and her staff the new owners generally renamed their new pet as they saw fit. It was only to be expected and, personally, I wouldn't have wanted it otherwise. But once (and once only) I discovered an exception to the rule when I rescued a dog that had been trapped down an old mineshaft near Hapton. She was a young collie cross, black and white with a long coat and a brilliant temperament. After I had secured her at the base of the shaft, she licked me all over as I held her in my arms on our journey to the top courtesy of the local fire lads and some volunteer helpers. I took her to the shelter and Sylvia recognized her instantly. 'It's Effie. Definitely. You brought her in as an abandonment from Burnley. Remember?'

'Yes . . . I do now.'

'We'll have a record of the people we rehomed her with in the office. They'll have changed her name, though.' Slowly, it all came back to me and I recalled naming her after a character in the Sherlock Holmes story 'The Yellow Face'.

Effie was traced to the Smith family on Rossendale Road, Burnley, and reunited with them. They had actually kept the name I'd given their dog and in that respect, to my knowledge, they were unique during all my years of service.

One bright summer's day I got a call to rescue a young crow hanging from a TV aerial on top of a four-storey block of flats in Blackburn. When I arrived the unfortunate bird was clearly visible for miles around. What looked like a metre of black cord or twine was wrapped round its left leg at one end and the aerial on top of the chimney at the other. The crow was flapping about pathetically in a vain attempt to free itself but was rapidly becoming exhausted. Something had to be done quickly.

I knocked on the door of the fourth-floor flat that seemed nearest to the location and asked if I might take a look out of their bedroom window. The elderly couple were obliging and within a few minutes I was hanging precariously out of the window while I assessed the situation. I had hoped to net the bird from there but the distance was too great. I couldn't see any alternative, in the circumstances, to asking the fire brigade to attend. I never liked calling them out unless it was unavoidable. Generally, they had their work cut out without me on the blower wanting help as well. I have to say, though, that the fire lads always turned out for me and many a time their assistance proved invaluable.

Usually, this sort of incident ended up as a ladder job, but this time the officer in charge of Blue Watch decided a Simon Snorkel should be brought into action. It sounds like the name of a cartoon character but in fact it's the hydraulic aerial platform used by the fire brigarde to rescue people. Edging the big vehicle into position by the side of the flats was a nightmare, and I'm afraid there was some damage to a couple of gardens in the process. Fortunately, when there's an animal in distress, people can be remarkably cooperative, I've found. I once knocked a good-sized hole in a couple's kitchen wall trying to locate and rescue a bird in the cavity between the brickwork. They urged me on without complaint. I've turned up brand new carpets, mangled floorboards, turned lofts into war zones. Witnessing the incredible tolerance exhibited by the owners of the properties was, well, humbling. Their sole concern at the time was for the trapped dog, cat, or bird. What they thought later as they surveyed the carnage is anyone's guess, but full marks to the public in general in those rescue situations.

I accompanied two of the firemen in the cage as we were manoeuvred over the rooftop and towards the chimney where the bird was hanging helplessly from the TV aerial. We had a superb view and I could clearly see the tall town hall building, Ewood Park, the football ground, the moors over to isolated Pickup Bank and, much nearer, the busy railway station.

I had two sets of extending grasper rods with me and, with a knife attached to the end of one of them, I tried to cut the line between bird and aerial, having placed the second set of rods with a net attached under the crow. Unfortunately, the knife wasn't strong enough, operating at a distance, to sever the twine or cord. It was time to return to the ground and think again. Somehow the link between bird and aerial had to be broken but we couldn't get any nearer to it than nine or ten feet so it wasn't going to be easy.

I was looking across at the firemen when I had a sudden brainwave.

'Hey, lads. I know you carry all sorts of equipment. Have you got a blowtorch with you?' I asked hopefully. One of the men went off to the cab of the fire engine and returned with the item.

'What's the big idea?' he enquired.

'That twine or cord. I couldn't cut it, so let's burn through it.' I used a length of spare rope to strap the blowtorch to the end of the grasper in place of the knife. Finally, we were ready to go. We must have made a strange sight as we ascended – two grinning firemen plus an RSPCA man with a blowtorch on the end of a pole. We were certainly attracting a crowd and the natives gathered in great numbers to watch the free show.

Cameras flashed but weren't that flash themselves in those pre-digital days. Video cameras were unknown to the public, though, oddly, not to me. I had a friend at UMIST (the University of Manchester Institute of Science and Technology) where work on their development was ongoing. We visited him one night at his house in Chadderton and he showed us a prototype they were working on, which he'd almost certainly brought home without authorization. It was a huge, heavy, ugly-looking thing and about as user-friendly as auto-electrics. We still have a five-minute black and white tape we made that evening long before video cameras reached the market place.

With difficulty, in the limited room available in the Snorkel's cage, I once again manoeuvred the set of rods with the net attachment under the bird. Then I screwed together the second set of rods and lit the blowtorch, which promptly blew out again. I had to reel the thing back towards me and light it four times in all before I got lucky. Working quickly, I managed to position the flame next to the twine or cord that was holding the bird fast.

Much to my relief it burned through in seconds and the crow dropped neatly into the net below.

When we finally returned to the ground the crowd cheered while I examined the bird, which was exhausted and in a state of shock. Fortunately, everything seemed fine except for some chafing where the cord, as it turned out to be, had rubbed against the crow's leg. The damage wasn't excessive and nothing to worry about unduly. I cleaned the area before placing him in a carrier in my van, then went back and asked Blue Watch for their details to include on a rescue report. Normally, I didn't bother with these as I always regarded rescuing animals as part of the job and not as a means of accumulating commendations and medals. However, if I'd been assisted by others I filled in a report on their behalf so that they received due recognition for their efforts.

I kept Colin, as Kathie named him, for over twenty-four hours till he'd fully recovered from his ordeal and was eating and drinking well. I released him early in the morning in the vicinity of the block of flats. With a deal of satisfaction I watched as he took off and became a small black dot on the horizon. How many folk get job satisfaction like that? I felt light headed, as if I'd had a few pints down the local though it was barely 5.30 a.m. I could smell the sweetness in the air and almost taste the dew. The world was about to wake up, but Colin and I were already experiencing life to the full. We were ahead of the game and I wondered again how I ever got to be so lucky.

# FIFTEEN

Although the system of individual inspectors working branch areas was a long-established and largely successful one, around 1976 the first moves towards dividing inspectors into groups throughout the country, each headed by a group chief inspector, were put into place. Geography, manpower and other local or regional concerns determined the size of the groups, which varied from five to fourteen or fifteen inspectors in places like London, Birmingham and Manchester. I became part of the Manchester group, though I could be said to be on its outer limits.

My group chief inspector was Des Pratt who'd recently been promoted, or made up as we used to say, after several failed attempts over the years. At first, I couldn't see why the powers that be hadn't promoted him a lot earlier. As time passed, though, I began to appreciate that Des had a few flaws. The fast-talking Welshman had recourse to what he called the Ways and Means Act far too often for my liking. He also had his own interpretation of the term 'group meeting', which surely wasn't what headquarters and the chief officer had in mind. Every four to six weeks Des would call a group meeting and it was always at the same venue: the Whip and Yelp public house, in Jeff Knowles the Bury inspector's area.

There were nine of us then in the Manchester group and nine vans would arrive around noon in the Yelp's car park on the day of a meeting. They were generally in a clean, well-maintained condition. Inspectors had private use of their vehicles and they naturally took pride in their appearance. In those days, petrol for private use was paid for by the individual inspector and a weekly return sent to headquarters. When we occasionally railed against low wages we were told that the perk of having the use of the Society's vehicle when off duty was the reason that wages weren't higher. It seemed a reasonable argument, until the taxman decided we had to pay five hundred pounds annually for the privilege. In the circumstances, some small increase in salary might have been expected. We never saw a penny. Strange, that. But none of us had joined up to get rich and we got on with it as usual.

Des Pratt chaired the jolly get-togethers as we supped our pints of Boddies bitter. It was all quite informal, more like meeting friends for a lunchtime drink than anything else, but I always began to feel uneasy as 3 p.m. approached. Something wasn't quite right. People don't put money in collecting boxes or leave legacies to the Society to see front-line workers relaxing with a pint in the pub for hours on end. It wasn't as if anything much was achieved by the meetings, although Des insisted they were good team-building exercises. As we weren't really a team in the true sense I couldn't see the point. However, at one of these group meetings Des, for once, had something of interest to announce.

'Right, lads, listen up, will you? I've had a request . . .'

'I know. But you still haven't paid for a round.'

'Thank you, Jeff. This request . . .'

'Sounds serious,' said Ged.

'It is, boyo. It's from Martin Egan, the chief of the Liverpool group.'

'Money or men?' queried Jeff. 'It'll be one or the other with Martin.'

'You're right. It's men he's after,' said Des. 'There aren't enough in Liverpool, it seems.'

'Well, if the women are complaining and want to give me a call I'd be glad to pop over for an evening or two,' offered Paul Simmons from Wigan.

'They're not that desperate!' said Ged. There was an outburst of laughter before the chief could continue.

'Now. Any of you lot fancy a day at the races?' He looked round at a sea of blank faces.

'When and where?' asked Paul.

'It's the Grand National at Aintree, isn't it? The Thursday, Friday and Saturday of the meeting. Martin needs one of us on the first two days and two on the Saturday when it's the big race. Come on . . . who's up for it then? Overtime for the Saturday lads and all.'

I put in for the Saturday along with Ged and we arranged

to meet at his house and travel to Liverpool together in his van. It turned out to be one hectic twenty-four hours. A call on the Friday afternoon began the merry-go-round. It concerned two oiled swans on a lodge at Victoria Street, Accrington. Sadly, I arrived to find the cob dead on the bank, almost certainly through ingesting oil while preening. The pen was circling nearby on the polluted water, obviously distressed and covered in oil like her dead partner. She needed to be caught quickly or, in all likelihood, she'd suffer the same fate.

Luckily, a car repair firm which occupied part of the old mill premises adjoining the lodge had a small rowing boat. One of their grease monkeys offered to take the oars and we drifted in silently through the slick of oil to within a few yards of the swan. We caught her with little difficulty, which showed that she was already experiencing the effects of the oil. There was a token attempt to evade us but any real fight had been knocked out of her already, and I held her tight to my chest till we were back on dry land and I could examine her more closely. It was heavy oil and would take a lot of time, care and patience to remove, during which the shock to her system of being repeatedly handled, however gently, and the danger from ingesting oil through attempts at preening would threaten her survival. Still, I thought it was worth a try and landed her back home around teatime.

'Egg and chips,' announced Kathie, as I stepped into the kitchen.

'Is it ready yet?'

'Five minutes. Why?'

'I've something in the van.' She looked at me with the familiar mix of exasperation and resignation that cooks experience on a daily basis trying to provide meals for kids, unthinking adults who ought to know better and, especially, RSPCA inspectors who never finish duty on time.

'Go on. I'll hold things up.'

'Where's the little 'un?'

'In her playpen and trying, as usual, to get out of it.' I quickly looked in on her in the living room. As soon as she spotted me she tottered over to my side of the play-pen, arms outstretched in full 'rescue me, daddy' mode. I would have loved to, of course, but I knew if I did it would be almost impossible to land her back there again without tears and tantrums. I blew her a quick kiss and ducked back into the kitchen.

I was faced with a dilemma. The utility room was currently home to a gorgeous smoky grey cat and her four two-week-old kittens. Sylvia at the shelter had promised to take them in but not until Monday or Tuesday of next week and I needed somewhere immediately to keep the swan while I worked to remove the oil. The garage was the only option and I cleared everything out. Some stuff I crammed into the utility room, some in the loft and the rest in a small garden shed which had been earmarked for demolition by Kathie. I made a place for the swan to rest and provided bread and water – the latter in the shape of a large plastic child's paddling pool donated by Peter next door. It was the best I could do for the time being. The idea was to let her rest and start on the cleaning-up process after my trip to Aintree.

I explained the situation to Kathie over tea and she offered to look after and feed the swan for me while I was at the races. I knew it would be difficult to judge how much and how often to clean her in order to minimize shock. Only washing-up liquid could be used as more effective chemicals, Benzene and the like, were far too strong and dangerous. So I ended up with a swan in my garage and the van on the drive again. Crazy . . . but Kathie and I were young, on a mission and just loving life.

Early on the morning of the Grand National I arrived at Ged's house in Bolton dead on time.

'Sorry, Steve. I'll just be a few minutes,' he said. 'I've promised the missus kippers for breakfast in bed and I'm running a bit late.' A little later I spotted two strips of leather and a cup of weak tea being rapidly transferred upstairs to his unfortunate wife. Well, it's the thought that counts, I suppose.

'Ready?' he said, rejoining me outside.

'Have you got any more of those kippers, Ged?'

'Why?'

'Three or four more like those and you'd have enough for a lovely leather belt, mate.'

We set off for Liverpool down the East Lancs Road and arrived just in time for a briefing by the Society's equine consultant, Superintendent Bob Stamford. Over the years, as the RSPCA's representative in talks with those in charge of the National, he has probably done more than anyone to make the course safer for the many horses taking part each year. Improvements to fences, including the dangerous Becher's Brook, have been major achievements. So has the increasing emphasis on animal welfare at top level.

Bob distributed hand-held radios so we could communicate with each other wherever we were on the course. Basically, our role was to deter any maltreatment or abuse of the horses and, should there be an incident at the fence we were manning, to assist the vet and stewards to restrain and rescue the animals involved. Incidents were to be reported promptly to Bob, who would make the final decision on any necessary action to be taken.

Fifteen inspectors and a couple of chiefs piled into a tired old Transit van and headed across Liverpool for Aintree. Crowds were flocking in and around the course in their thousands. Initially, at least, it was a fine day as the sun came out and temperatures hovered around the 18 degree mark. But, even then, dark patches of cloud blotted the blue sky, indicating a change in the weather sooner or later. That was always a problem on duty at the early April Grand National meetings – you never knew whether summer or winter uniform should be the order of the day. If you put your coat on to walk to a fence it would generally turn out fine and warm. Leave your coat off and the heavens would open and you'd get a soaking for certain. The weather forecasters called it changeable. We called it something along the lines of 'a bugger'.

Once inside the confines of the course, having survived

the strict security checks at our entrance gate, the van pulled up a hundred yards along the track in the direction of the grandstand away in the distance. It was already pretty full, awash with celebrities and film stars with egos as big as their hats. I eventually tore my eyes away from the great and the good and it was then that I noticed the caravan. Or at least something resembling one. It's no exaggeration to say that it made Ged's look like a top of the range model. There are depths of dilapidation and neglect and this beauty plumbed them all. Along with the whole group, I was hoping it wouldn't turn out to be our accommodation and, along with the whole group, I was sadly disappointed. More than a few remarks followed.

'Blood and thunder! Call that a caravan?'

'How old is it? And how is it still standing?'

'The tyres are flat and it's leaning at an angle.'

'Most of the windows are cracked or broken. We'll have to keep our coats on in there.'

'There's probably a caveman living in it!'

Bob Stamford, looking sheepish it has to be said, called for order.

'Now then, lads. Let's keep a sense of proportion. It's not as bad inside as you might think.'

'It couldn't be,' Jeff Knowles agreed.

'As I said,' continued Bob, 'it's a little belter inside. And what's more, it didn't cost the earth . . .'

'You mean you shelled out for it? Folding notes, coins of the realm, that sort of thing?' enquired an incredulous Billy McKay from Barrow.

'Well, it was the best one in the scrapyard.'

'*What?*'

Bob burst out laughing. 'Only a joke, lads. Only a joke. Now . . . try it out for size and stop whingeing.' With everyone piled inside it was standing room only and Ged and I were lucky to get a seat with a ripped cushion. The only positive was the fact that the thing had a stove that somehow still worked, and mugs of steaming hot tea began to circulate among us, lifting our punctured morale.

Ged and I looked outside down the track. The nearby caravan of the St John's Ambulance Brigade was larger and in much better nick but it wasn't just the caravan that attracted our attention. Framed in a window, two of their girls were having a laugh and giving us the eye in no uncertain manner. Ged's reaction was to blow them a kiss while I buried my head in an ancient copy of the *Daily Mirror* someone had left behind.

'Pack it in, will you?' I muttered. 'They might get the wrong idea.'

'Mine's a looker,' he replied, 'and I think she's ahead of you.'

Bob told us which fences everyone would be manning during the day. There were several races round the smaller Mildmay course prior to the National itself, which would start around 3.45 p.m. Maps were issued to help us pinpoint our designated fences and two of us were allocated the additional duty of checking parked cars for dogs left inside. Even at outside temperatures as moderate as 20 degrees centigrade, the animals could be in dire straits.

Half an hour before the first race a buzz went round the course that royalty was arriving.

'Not the Queen, is it?' I speculated.

'Probably Charlie,' surmised Ged.

Billy McKay from Barrow gave Bob Stamford a dirty look. 'I wonder what his caravan's like?' he said, and we all burst out laughing. Jeff Knowles nearly choked on the remains of a wine gum he was sucking.

'Hey, Ged,' I said. 'I take it all back. . . what I said about your caravan.'

He looked offended. 'My mobile home, you mean.'

'Right. I – I thought bad thoughts, me old mate. I'm seeing things in a new light now.' Ged grinned and pulled out a pack of twenty Park Drive.

'Smoking's not allowed inside the caravan,' Bob told us.

'It's starting to rain,' Billy complained.

'You should be used to it where you come from,' exclaimed 'little' Alec Minshull, a six-foot-six-inch giant with a squeaky voice and excessive nasal hair who worked the Macclesfield area.

'Oh, I'm used to it all right,' agreed Billy. 'But I've never grown to like it.'

During the periods in the caravan in between races almost every topic under the sun got an airing as the lads, papers all read, tried to fend off boredom. I got round to discussing a famous unsolved Liverpool murder with one of their lads, Tony Pollard, who knew the city inside out having worked the area for ten years or more. The Wallace case has been described as 'unbeatable' and so it is. Almost every known fact in the affair can be viewed as further establishing the guilt of the accused, William Herbert Wallace, or as helping to demolish the case against him, depending on your point of view.

On the night of the murder Wallace went searching for an address in the Allerton district, which he barely knew as he lived in Anfield on the other side of the city. His search for Menlove Gardens East proved fruitless. Not surprisingly, as it did not exist. There were certainly Menlove Gardens North, South and West, I told Tony, but no East.

'No. You're wrong there,' he said. Now, I knew that I was 100 per cent right having studied the case for many years, so I claim no great credit for sticking to my guns and insisting that there was, for sure, no Menlove Gardens East in the city and never had been. Nevertheless, Tony swore he knew better.

'I was round there last week on a call. I definitely saw Menlove Gardens East. I remember.'

'I'm sorry, Tony, but you're wrong. There's no East.'

'But I saw it!'

'Must have been hot in Liverpool that day.'

'What do you mean?'

'Well, you saw a mirage. Like in the desert.'

He reached deep into his trouser pocket and produced a ten-pound note. 'This says I'm right, Stevie boy.'

'And I say you're wrong.'

'Match it then.'

'I'm not going to take your money when I know for certain you're going to lose.'

He gave me a sneering, exasperated look. 'Keep on clucking!'

'Listen, mate. Go and get a street map of Liverpool from your van. I'll be waiting here.'

He returned a few minutes later with the map – still confident, absolutely sure of the outcome. 'Okay, Steve. Last chance . . . I'll even make it twenty if you like. I can't say fairer than that.' I could see he wasn't going to take no for an answer and all the other lads had cottoned on to our conversation by then, interested to see who had it right.

'Look, Tony. Let it drop. What does it matter?'

The Liverpool lads started with the flapping arms and chicken noises which, I felt, were well out of order. I thought it out for a moment or two.

'I'll tell you what,' I said. 'If there's a Menlove Gardens East . . .'

'No if about it. I told you, I saw it last week.'

'Yes. All right. If there is an East, I'll pay up double the twenty quid. If not, we'll call it quits – no money exchanged.' He shook his head, followed by my hand, and then opened the map at a page detailing the Mossley Hill and Allerton districts of Liverpool. Gradually, the mile-wide smile on his face began to fade and soon he was frantically scanning the map for what he knew to be there – only it wasn't. Beforehand, most of the others in the group would have put their money on Tony so there were some surprised looks and remarks when he was seen to be struggling.

'He'll find it.'

'He's all hyped up. Probably missed it first time round.'

'Come on, Tone.' Tone was now scouring the index of street names at the back of the map book.

'Give up?' I asked him.

'No. It has to be here.' I left him to it and stepped outside the caravan for some fresh air. After a quarter of an hour spent consulting his mates' maps as well as checking his own again he had to admit defeat. He came out of the caravan and joined me on the Melling Road.

'I'm gobsmacked, Stevie. I was absolutely certain, but it's not on the map. As you said, there's North, South and West but not East. How were you so sure?'

'I've studied the case on and off for years, and walked all the streets and all.'

'But I work Mossley Hill. I've been all round Menlove Avenue and that district numerous times. I would have sworn in court that I'd been on Menlove Gardens East.'

'Well, if you have, you'd better change your name to Qualtrough,' I said, walking back to the caravan.

'Qualtrough . . . Why?'

'Read the book . . . Jonathan Goodman's *The Killing of Julia Wallace*.'

The first few races went off without any real problems although the radios didn't always perform as expected. Mine was okay most of the time but sometimes, without warning, it would tune itself into Radio Albania or the like at a volume that threatened to perforate an unsuspecting eardrum.

At 3.15 in the afternoon the caravan emptied and we all headed off to our fences for the National itself. Ged had been allocated Becher's Brook and Jeff Knowles Valentine's. Alec Minshull was covering the Chair while I'd drawn fence five – the one before Becher's. The rain had eased from earlier in the afternoon and it was quite warm in an all-weather coat as the sun shone down gloriously.

'We can't go on meeting like this. People will talk.' It was one of the St John's girls who'd been checking us out from the window of their caravan earlier. 'What's your name then?'

'Steve.'

'I'm Brenda. Do you want to know a secret?'

'McCartney and Lennon composition. Big hit for Billy J. Kramer and the Dakotas in 1963. Later, the credits on Beatles tracks were changed to the more familiar Lennon and McCartney.'

She looked at me in shock. 'I'm talking about my friend Sandra . . . she fancies you rotten.'

'Really?'

'Like I say.'

With a certain amount of foreboding I asked her where her mate was.

'The first fence.'

Short of Sandra's having drawn my fence, it was a worst-case scenario. We had ladies' man Ray Rawstron on that one and Randy Ray plus Sizzling Sandra sounded positively inflammatory when I thought about it – which was all too briefly, because just then the race started.

Before there was time to blink the runners and riders, minus a few early fallers, were nearly upon us. Standing there at the side of that fence the thunderclap of forty or so horses passing close by at speed was a whole new and positively alarming experience. The word awesome is used all too frivolously these days but the formidable noise of that Grand National field really was jaw-droppingly awesome and stays with me to this day. Both animal and jockey put their lives on the line in National Hunt racing and disaster is always one stumble, one mistake, away. That was a fact deeply impressed on me that afternoon at Aintree. While I admit there is something noble, magnificent and, yes, grand about the whole thing – particularly the courage exhibited by both horses and men – I have to wonder whether the whole flamboyant, inherently dangerous spectacle is worth the inevitable occasional carnage.

I was weighing everything up in my mind when it became clear that help was needed at Becher's. The sloping ground on the landing side usually causes trouble, and there'd been several well-fancied fallers. Most of the horses and jockeys had escaped unhurt but one horse was lying on its side a few yards clear of the fence. The course vet, two stewards and Ged were struggling to calm and restrain the animal. I arrived on the scene at the same time as Aintree's horse ambulance, but before any effective action could be taken by anyone Keeper's Pantry died. The jockey, himself cut and limping badly, arrived a few minutes later. Taking in the scene at a glance he turned away in tears, his head bowed low.

Ged and I walked slowly back in the general direction of the caravan. The big race now over, there was a muted buzz around Aintree and some of the peacocks and posers who were not there primarily for the racing had started to leave. My knowledge of the sport of kings is not extensive but racing certainly attracts some bizarre punters with very deep pockets and, apparently, no great desire to hang on to their hard-earned money. Or maybe it comes too easily to them in the first place. I don't know. Ged and I walked on in silence, both of us still affected by the tragic death of Keeper's Pantry at Becher's. Then I remembered.

'Ged.'

'What?'

'I was talking to Brenda, one of those St John's girls at the window. She was on my fence.'

'You lucky blighter.'

'Will you listen?'

'I'm all ears, Steve.'

'She told me her mate—'

'—Fancies you, I know. What's new?'

'No. Not that.'

'That sky's gone dark all of a sudden,' he said. 'Looks like it might rain soon. Let's get a shift on.' We speeded up but I resumed the conversation.

'Brenda told me that her mate Sandra had drawn the first fence.'

'So what?'

'Think about it.'

Suddenly, Ged stopped in his tracks. 'Hey . . . isn't that Ray Rawstron's fence?'

'You're getting there.'

'You don't think he . . . and her . . . and him . . . together . . . ?'

'Well, it's a possibility.'

'Randy Ray Rawstron and your little raver . . . never.
Mind you, he's a bit of a lad, a chancer, is Ray. Then
there's that empty caravan.'

'With torn curtains. But they'd probably suffice.' We
broke into a trot.

'He'd make do, would Ray,' said Ged. 'Hurry!'

Our rapid progress meant we were within a hundred
yards of the Melling Road when a deep, booming voice
brought us to a halt.

'Greenhalgh . . . Hardwick. Hold up. Wait for me.' It
was the man in charge, equine consultant and travelling
superintendent Bob Stamford. Positively the last person, in
view of our suspicions, that we wanted to meet just then.
Bob led the way and a few other colleagues joined us. On
the edge of the Melling Road were half a dozen more of
our group standing and staring at something across the
way. Ray Rawstron wasn't among them. With their backs
to us they had no inkling that Bob was around and within
hearing distance.

'Look at that!'

'I'm looking.'

'Would you Adam and Eve it?'

'Anything's possible knowing Ray.'

'Yes . . . but this is the limit even for him.'

'Blimey! Good job old Bob's not around. That lad would
be out on his ear and no mistake.'

'But I am around,' boomed Bob, as we closed in on them from behind. 'What's all this about?' He hadn't been able to see what they were staring at till the group fell apart on his arrival. Then, suddenly, everything became crystal clear. The old caravan was rocking on its base of flat tyres and broken bricks. There was movement inside of a pretty energetic nature and the same thought was in all our minds, including Bob's, regarding the cause of it.

'Where's Ray Rawstron?' he said, only to be met by shrugged shoulders and blank expressions. 'Has anyone seen him after the finish of the race?' No one had. Just then the chap in charge of the St John's ambulance crew hurried over. He seemed agitated.

'Have you seen one of our girls, Sandra Bingham? She's not come back from the first fence. We're starting to get worried . . .' His voice trailed off as he clocked the caravan. 'Looks like there's a party going on over there.' Momentarily, he seemed bemused. Then it dawned on him too. 'You don't think . . .'

'We shouldn't jump to conclusions,' said Bob in a low voice.

'Are any of your lads missing?' asked the St John's man. Our faces gave him his answer. 'Well?'

'We do have a man unaccounted for at the moment,' began Bob, putting his best spin on it.

'Aye. Randy Ray Rawstron,' announced Billy McKay unhelpfully. 'He was on the first fence too.'

'What? Am I to understand this . . . this Randyman

was with Sandra at the first fence and now they are both missing?'

'There's no evidence . . .' began Bob.

'What's that then?' the St John's man interrupted, pointing at the rocking caravan.

'We'll see,' said Bob, striding out at the head of what had become a small uniformed army of RSPCA inspectors and St John's ambulance staff.

As we neared the caravan puzzled looks spread among the party. The scuffling and shuffling sounds and the general kerfuffle seemed very odd, if not positively weird. For a couple intent on a clandestine liaison they were behaving erratically to say the least. The situation had been brought to the attention of the racecourse staff and two senior stewards had joined the merry throng as Bob Stamford grabbed the door handle and pushed it down. The door flew open, revealing . . . a couple of playful young lurchers but no sign of human occupation.

'What the blazes . . .' began Bob, as he was bowled over by the two dogs. They almost licked him to death as he sprawled in a heap on the ground outside the caravan. The relief on our faces turned to laughter as we watched Bob struggle to his feet and stumble unsteadily towards our waiting hands. Someone herded the over-affectionate lurchers back inside and closed the door, leaving everyone to wonder exactly where they'd come from and who had put them in the caravan.

I felt a pull on my coat sleeve followed by a hoarse, insistent voice not much above a whisper. 'Them dogs is all right, sir. You can see they're well fed an' all.' I looked round to see a small dark man wearing an ill-fitting flat cap and a grubby white muffler. He looked worried.

'They're in good bodily condition, certainly,' I replied.

'Ah, so you agree then?'

'Of course. But that's not the point.'

He looked, if possible, even more worried. 'Not the p-p-point?' he stuttered. 'What's the point then, sir, if it's not their condition? Sure, what is the bloomin' point if it's not that?' He was no longer whispering, and for some reason his dander was up. I began to take him seriously.

'What's your interest in those dogs then?' I demanded.

'Interest, is it? It'd be a fine thing if a man wasn't interested in what's his own.'

'You own them?'

'They're God's creatures,' said the little man, 'but I look to them down here like.'

'What's your name?'

'Fearghal O'Flaherty . . . The first, the worst and the only.' I made a note of it in my book, called Bob over and explained the situation as best I could. He looked fit to explode as he looked the little man in the eye.

'What do you mean by it? What in the world possessed you to put your dogs, if they are yours, in our caravan?'

'I thought it was derelic', didn't I? It was handy while I went for a jimmy riddle and put a bet on.'

'Derelic'!' howled Bob, his pumped-up red face a picture. That was it . . . everyone collapsed laughing.

'Well, it does look like it,' countered one of the course

stewards. 'I nearly had it towed away myself!' The laughter swelled and some people had tears in their eyes. Fearghal opened the door of the caravan and the dogs were all over him, tails wagging furiously in recognition.

'Ah, me beauties! Sorry I am to have put you in that place but I was burstin' an' all.'

Bob Stamford was speechless. Fearghal was feted and, at least for the rest of the afternoon, became something of a folk hero. We were left wondering where Ray Rawstron and his St John's lass had got to. Not five minutes later he arrived alone at a brisk walking pace, calm as you like.

'Where in blazes have you been?' yelled Bob.

Ray looked startled. 'Sorry! I . . . I had a little bet on with Sandra and I've just been collecting the winnings.'

'Sandra, I take it, being the St John's girl on your fence. Where is she now?'

'Back at their caravan. I think her boss is giving her a hard time. He's not as understanding as you, Bob – you having a bit of a flutter too, eh?'

Bob's face suddenly took on a beetroot-like aspect. He knew Ray had him in his pocket. He could hardly put the lad on a 'fizzer', a formal disciplinary charge, for doing what he'd done himself. Thoroughly exasperated, he tramped off to smoke a calming cigar by the Melling Road.

'You're one lucky lad,' I told Ray.

'Luck – nah! And it's not who you know either. It's *what* you know!'

There were two more races left to cover at the National meeting before we could leave. The penultimate race saw

One in a Crowd pull up sharply with a leg problem and we sent for our own horse ambulance as Aintree's was busy elsewhere. While we were calming him down with the vet in attendance, edging the animal tentatively towards the ambulance, an ear-piercing siren began to wail and got louder as a line of policemen appeared and came striding purposefully towards us. One in a Crowd reacted badly and all our good work so far was undone. A large Neanderthal-type officer addressed us at the top of his voice. 'You lot shift!' We were stunned by the words and even more so by his attitude. Bob pointed out that we were dealing with an injured horse.

'Never mind the bloody horse!'

'But we need to get him into the ambulance,' explained Billy McKay.

'Move yourselves and quick. Prince Charles wants to leave. If you don't shift and pronto you'll all be arrested!'

'What?' said Billy. 'The horse and all?'

The lame horse and our ambulance had to be dragged to one side and we were made to wait. About ten minutes later the royal Range Rover, driven at speed, flashed by. Presumably, though the windows were too dark to see, it contained the heir to the throne and his immediate entourage. The incident, on the surface unfeeling and totally unnecessary, left a nasty taste in the mouth amongst all who were present that day.

'Never mind the horse, indeed.'

'Poor beggar can suffer if it gets in Charlie's way.'

'That's well out of order.'

One in a Crowd went on to make a full recovery and earn a substantial amount of money over the next few seasons for his owner, Mrs Slingsby-Pocklington, so no great harm was done. And to be fair, Prince Charles himself might have had no knowledge of the incident. Nevertheless, at Aintree that year the monarchy scored *nul points*, equalling the usual score of Britain's entry in the Eurovision song contest. He would probably have delayed his exit from the course if someone had told him there was good reason to.

Unexpectedly, our Aintree accommodation achieved a certain amount of fame, not to say notoriety. That evening, though I missed the programme myself, there was a repeat broadcast of the big race featuring extra footage filmed by the BBC cameras before and after the National. They had picked out our caravan and lingered. Inevitably, it became the subject of some speculation and dry humour by the commentary team though, luckily, they had no idea that it belonged to the Society.

That should have been the end of it, but a local newspaper cutting arrived a few days later from Liverpool. It was headlined, FIRE AT AINTREE STAMPED OUT. Apparently, before it could be towed away, the caravan had suffered an arson attack by person or persons of impeccable taste during the night. It's wrong to point the finger at anyone with no evidence of guilt at all, but if I ever meet up again with Mr Feargal O'Flaherty – the first, the worst and the only – it would be interesting to question him as to his whereabouts on the night our caravan burned down.

# SIXTEEN

It was nine in the evening when I finally landed home after duty at the National. Kathie was exhausted and half asleep when I found her in the living room. She'd been reading Tolkien's *Lord of the Rings* but the uncomfortably thick volume had slipped out of her grasp and was lying open on the floor at her feet.

'Sorry I'm late,' I began. 'Did you see me on TV?'

'No. You weren't on *The Generation Game* that I remember.'

'Idiot! At the National. I was on the fence before Becher's.'

'Must have been painful squatting high up on a pile of old Christmas trees.'

'Right, Mrs . . .' I resorted to my usual ploy whenever Kathie got sarky and exploited her ultimate weakness – ticklishness. A frenetic few minutes followed that ended with her glass of lemonade broken and our small beech-wood drinks table upturned over a wet carpet.

'You daft bugger!' she growled, trying to keep her voice down. Emma was asleep.

'It was your fault,' I insisted.

'What?'

'Being so grumpy.'

'You . . . you . . .' I collapsed next to her and, within minutes, we were both sound asleep with our arms round each other on the sofa.

The next morning I padded downstairs to the kitchen and made us a cup of tea. Kathie had been joined by Emma when I returned. She was playing with an old hairbrush and was wide awake. I handed Kathie her cuppa and we all ended up playing Snap for ages.

Later, I looked in on the swan in the garage. She seemed settled enough for the time being, and when I heard the telephone ring I headed back into the house.

I was off duty that Sunday but Ged had asked if I could cover for him between midday and 2 p.m. as he'd some family business to sort out with his brother. Working in partnership with a neighbouring inspector as most of us did, it was usually no problem to accommodate things like that. There was a commitment to your branch area and your closest colleague that was lost later when the emphasis changed to a group system. It was Murphy's law, though, that an urgent call would come in during the coverage period and, of course, one did.

It was a woman's voice on the end of the line and she was obviously close to tears though she was actually calling on a neighbour's behalf. At first, I couldn't make sense of her story, but with questioning it became clearer. Apparently, her neighbour's dog had gone out that morning and had come back covered in tar. The owner was an elderly man, Alfred Furness, of Plover Street, Bolton, in Ged's area. Normally, with an owned animal, I would have advised a vet be contacted and arranged some financial help if needed, but the woman told me the old chap was housebound, hadn't a penny to spare and his dog meant the world to him. If it was a sob story then it was one I felt I couldn't ignore and I agreed to visit within the hour.

I put on my uniform, including a nice crisply ironed shirt courtesy of Kathie, and made a flask of coffee as I usually did when I trespassed into Ged's area. Then I set off in my dark blue Escort van (yes, I do remember the reg – OUF 406M). I knew the main arterial road between Blackburn and Bolton, the A666, was littered with roadworks so I decided to take the longer, more scenic route along by the Strawberry Duck Inn at Entwistle and then on to Edgworth where I could rejoin the A666 on the other side of the works.

The plan was successful and I passed through some beautiful moorland and countryside popular with walkers from miles around. Northern industrial towns are often thought of as grey and grim. Even accepting that, which is far from the truth, it's forgotten that they are frequently surrounded by areas of great natural beauty. Not two miles from Accrington, itself blessed with the coppice area overlooking the town, is Mill Hill – all stream, rocks and ravine – rarely bettered for a mildly challenging but stunningly scenic walk. Mushrooms are plentiful along the way if you know the right ones to pick and wild flowers decorate the fringes and stand proud and colourful in the wooded areas. If it's been raining the stream widens in parts and can become quite deep but there are plenty of places to cross safely and easily. Kathie and I had often walked there and we went back as a family when Emma came along.

I pulled up in Plover Street outside Mr Furness's house. The street itself was neat, clean and still partially cobbled, the old setts gleaming as they dried out after a light shower earlier. Most of the terraced houses looked sprightly and well maintained. Mr Furness's was among the exceptions, looking tired with peeling paintwork and the odd tile missing on the roof. Stepping out of the vehicle, I heard a brass band somewhere playing the Beatles' classic 'Hey Jude' and it sounded quite superb.

I knocked on the front door, which was answered by a middle-aged woman wrapped in a large red and white spotted pinny. Under her hairnet her brown hair was in curlers and she wore old-fashioned short white socks and clogs on her feet. I suddenly felt as if I'd stepped back in time to when I was a youngster in Oldham surrounded by mills and mill workers dressed in similar fashion.

'Come in, inspector. Thank God you're here.'

'Did you call us?'

'Yes. I'm Alice Tooley. I felt so sorry for Alfred when he showed me the dog.'

'Where do you live?'

'Across the road . . . number ninety-six. Come through to the living room.'

Alfred Furness was a tall, thin, frail man. He was seventy-two years old but still had a fine crop of snow-white hair. Curled up in an old armchair by an open fire when I came into the room, he rose and shook my hand with a firm, positive grip. His pale eyes flickered and his gaze led to a small Jack Russell lying wearily on a tattered strip of carpet directly in front of the fire. There were spots of heavy, clinging tar on its coat but it didn't seem anything to worry about. Then Alice Tooley lifted the dog up and I saw that the entire underside of the animal, including its nether regions, was covered in a thick layer of tar, which had set hard.

To say I'd never seen anything like it would be ridiculous, as I was relatively new to the job, but even in decades of service I never saw the like of it again. Where the tar had come from and how the dog had come to lie flat out in it was never explained.

'She went out this morning as usual,' said Mr Furness, 'and . . . and . . . came back like this. Oh, my God!'

'What's her name?' I asked.

'Queenie. My little Queenie. Is there anything you can do?'

'Don't worry, Mr Furness,' I said, knowing he had every reason to. 'Can I use your phone, Mrs Tooley?'

'Aye, follow me.'

I rang every veterinary practice in the Bolton area that Sunday and, unbelievably, none of them could see me with the dog. I gave up and contacted Halfords in Blackburn who simply asked what my estimated time of arrival might be. I told Mr Furness I was taking his dog to a vet and he could expect Queenie to be admitted for several days. He was upset, of course, and made it clear that 'money was a problem'. I told him not to worry on that score. Internal finances was an area where I found over the years that the Ways and Means Act I generally spurned came into its own and could be used to good effect.

Headquarters paid vet bills for the treatment of sick or injured unowned animals whilst the local branches, by means of issuing vouchers, paid at least part of the vet fees when owners couldn't afford the treatment. Wildlife in most cases received free veterinary attention. Nevertheless, there were always incidents and situations that refused to fit easily into any particular category and nobody thought they should pay.

Headquarters were also responsible for veterinary costs in cases reported for possible prosecution. These could be hefty invoices that included repeated consultations and further treatment costs plus fees for a vet's attendance at court. If I could foresee problems regarding responsibility for payment where, in my judgement, there was a deserving case I told the vet to add those costs, unacknowledged, to a prosecution job I might have ongoing with him at the time. Nobody got hurt and animals like Queenie got a chance of life, as otherwise euthanasia might have been the outcome – pretty much solely on financial grounds.

Local branches, to my mind correctly, liked to spread their resources around evenly, spending relatively small sums on a lot of different animals whose owners needed financial help rather than providing larger sums to assist fewer owners. Operations to rectify difficult long-term conditions or broken limbs were therefore out of the question. Kennelling and treating Queenie would inevitably require more funds than the branch usually made available. I decided, wrongly or rightly, that headquarters should go the extra mile for her and Alfred Furness, whether they knew they were doing it or not.

'It's going to cost a bit, young Steve,' Henry Halford told me. 'We'll keep it as low as a snake's belly for you, but . . .'

'I know, Henry. But I'm determined the dog will be put right for this chap. She's everything to him.'

He paused for thought. 'There's a way we can keep the costs down if you're not averse to a bit of old-fashioned elbow grease, Steve.'

'How's that?'

'Well we'll have first go at it and then you take her and continue the treatment.'

'What's the treatment?'

'Ether soap and, as I said, elbow grease. We'll provide you with enough of the soap to get by, and then you can bring her in again for a check and a final scrub and polish. It'll be hard work, mind.'

'We've an oiled swan that we're cleaning up, so the more the merrier,' I told him.

'Call back tomorrow afternoon for her then,' said Henry.

Fortunately, Sylvia at the animal shelter relieved me of the smoky grey cat and her kittens on Monday morning so the utility room was available for Queenie. I collected her from Halfords, along with the ether soap, as arranged. Progress had definitely been made and some areas of her coat where it had been possible had been shaved completely, but there was still a lot to do. Queenie herself was overjoyed to see me. Whether she'd feel the same after a couple of cleaning sessions was doubtful, but for a dog that was eight years old she was taking it well and never lost her appetite throughout it all.

Kathie had been helping me with the swan cleaning in the meantime and our lodger was now a much lighter shade of grey and, more important, still with us. The measures to minimize shock seemed to be working – at least for the time being.

I decided to contact Mr Furness and let him know everything was going well and it shouldn't be too long before Queenie was back home again. Unfortunately, Alice Tooley's phone line was out of action and I didn't want to bother Ged as I knew he was swamped with paperwork from three cases he had ongoing at the time. There was nothing for it but a quick trip to Bolton, a contradiction in terms really. I managed it on the Tuesday afternoon and knocked hard on Mr Furness's door in Plover Street, which was not far, I discovered, from the old Burnden Park football ground. There was no response.

'You'll need to knock hard, lad,' said the plump woman next door who'd come out at the sight of my van pulling up outside. 'Alf's a bit Mutt 'n' Jeff and his dog's not there at the moment. She usually lets him know if there's someone at the door.' I nodded and thumped the door hard with my fist and rapped my knuckles loudly on the woodwork. After a pause, shuffling footsteps could be heard approaching. Alfred Furness opened the door and his face lit up when he saw me.

'By heck! It's Inspector Greenhalgh. Have you got my Queenie with thee?'

'Not just yet, Mr Furness.'

'Nay . . . it's Alf, lad. Alf's the name.'

'Right . . . Alf. But don't worry. Another few days and she'll be back here right as rain.'

'That's grand, inspector.'

'It's Steve. Steve's the name,' I told him. He laughed and invited me into the house.

Once inside he slumped wearily into the threadbare armchair next to the feeble open fire. I sat further back in an equally well-worn chair. I noticed that a small, rickety bookcase in one corner had disappeared since my previous visit.

'Have you been selling furniture?' I enquired. He looked across at me sheepishly, almost shamefaced.

'Nay, lad. Burnin' it, yes. But sellin' it, no.' It was then that I noticed there were chunks of skirting board missing around the room.

'Have you no coal, Alf?'

'I've had a bit from Alice and t'others but it's run out.' I didn't like to dig deeper into his personal affairs, but clearly the old chap was living well below the poverty line if he'd been reduced to burning his furniture and fittings.

'Niver mind about me,' he said. 'Queenie's what matters.

Don't worry, Steve. There's food in theer for her all right.
She'll not go without.' He got up shakily, walked across
to the kitchen and opened a cupboard door. It was stuffed
full of tinned dog food and bags of dog biscuits. Then Alf
shuffled painfully back to his armchair by the fire, sat down
and warmed his hands. They were encased in a pair of
dark brown woollen gloves with the fingers cut short. He
moved gingerly as arthritis afflicted him and neither his
eyesight nor his hearing was the best. Outside, a gentle
rain began to fall and water promptly dripped through the
ceiling between the living room and the kitchen. It was my
first experience of real in-your-face poverty and, as such,
it made a lasting impression. When Alf offered to make
us a cup of tea he had to stop and think twice before he
was sure he had enough second-time-round tea bags left,
but somehow I knew it would have been wrong to refuse.
I had a fair bit of work on that day but I wanted to know
more about someone I'd gone out of my way to help so I
stayed a while.

'What did you do for a living, Alf?'

'Mainly coopering – makin' barrels and such. But the
trade was ailing and so was I. It were hard physical work
an' I had to give it up afore long.'

'How long?'

'Oh, nigh on twenty year.'

I smiled and gently shook my head. 'What about the
war?' His face set and he stared balefully into the flames of
the fire. 'What do you remember the most?'

There was no pause or hesitation. 'Dunkirk!' He'd been

at Dunkirk when the British Expeditionary Force of some 330,000 men was trapped on the French coast by the advancing German army. I asked him to tell me about it. He'd been an infantryman in the Lancashire Fusiliers in 1940, fighting in Belgium at Tournay. The Germans had forced the BEF to retreat to Lille and then, in disarray, towards the French coast.

'As we retreated, sharpish like, the order came that all soldiers dread . . . Every man for himself!'

'Really?'

'Aye. It amounts to officers abdicatin' their responsibility. There was terrible confusion and, eventually, I just followed the crowd towards the coast. Most stuck to the roads but there were enemy bombers and fighters strafing them so I took to the fields. I finally reached this beach somewhere near Dunkirk. It were called Bray Dunes and there were plenty of other lads stuck there – all of us sittin' ducks.'

'You thought you'd be killed, then?'

'Aye. Or taken prisoner. We were there four days. Then, at night, eight of us heard this shout from the direction of the sea . . . "Any of you so and so's know how to row?" We were too startled to reply at first, then a chorus of "No" went up. The voice started up again. "Well, now's the damn time to learn!" It was a naval rating with a rowboat and we rushed down to the water, spotted him and his boat through the gloom and piled in. Nine of us altogether in this small rowboat.'

'Go on, Alf,' I said, totally fascinated by his account.

'We're in the boat and the lad said, "Port. Starboard. Left. Right. When I say port, you on the left pull; when I say starboard, you on the right pull; when I say both, you all pull together. Got it?" We all nodded and got down to work. With good luck and his guidance we got through the breakers pushing us back to shore and came across a ship – a collier. We climbed up ropes that were hanging down the sides of her and landed on the deck exhausted. They put us in the hold and it were knee deep in coal dust. Filthy. You could hardly breathe down there. Still, we reached Blighty all right and that were that.'

'Most of the BEF were rescued, weren't they?'

'Aye. No thanks to them bloomin' officers who should have been in charge. They called it a miracle and I suppose it were.'

I have to admit I spent a couple of hours or more listening and chatting with Alf that day when I should have been on the road knocking on doors. He was so likeable and self-effacing. He told his story as if he was describing a trip to the supermarket. When I finally left, it was like leaving a good friend's and being rejuvenated by your visit. I decided to go home and get on with some more oil cleaning, be it Queenie or the swan.

It took rather longer than expected and a further visit to Halfords before Queenie could be returned to Alf, but the day finally arrived and both my wife and my daughter accompanied me when I made the trip back to Plover Street. Alice Tooley's phone had been repaired and I'd let her know when we were due. She'd told

Alf, who said he wouldn't believe it till he saw the little terrier again.

We pulled up at his front door to find a crowd of neighbours gathered round. A group of excited children ran inside the house and dragged a dozing Alf out of his armchair into the bright light of day. I carried Queenie out of the van and she went bananas on seeing Alf, struggling free from me and jumping into the old chap's open arms. It was quite a reunion and the neighbours joined in the celebrations with a spontaneous round of applause. There were still at least the remnants of a sense of true community in those late-seventies days, something almost entirely forgotten now. Back then, people still cared about, if not loved, their neighbours, and not in a nosy-parkering way but with goodwill and tolerance that often stretched to friendship. With tears in his eyes, Alf shook my hand. His other held the little dog, which was still excitedly licking her owner's face. Alf turned then and hugged both Kathie and Emma.

'I hear I've thee to thank too, lass,' he said to Kathie, 'for gettin' my Queenie right. That's a smashin' little 'un you've got. I've a lolly for her here and summat for thee, Steve.' Handing Queenie over temporarily to a neighbour, he pulled a red lolly in the shape of a spaceship, together with a large envelope, out of his coat pocket, and gave them to Emma and myself respectively. Then, with Queenie back in his arms, Alf gave a final wave to everyone and disappeared indoors. Before we left I tapped Alice Tooley on the shoulder. 'Look to him, will you, Alice . . . some more coal if he'll have it? If there's any more I can do, any time, let me know.' She nodded and headed home.

Em demolished the red lolly on the journey back in record time and, at our place over a cup of tea, we opened Alf's envelope. Inside was a handwritten manuscript detailing his service in the army, a letter and some personal effects. A note was attached.

> Thanks for everything. The letter's from Harry
> Grundy, a mate of mine. He rescued me when
> I got one in the belly. I was in no man's land
> at the time and I'd curled up to die when Harry
> arrived out of nowhere. He got me back behind
> our lines – how, I'll never know. Unfortunately,
> he died ten year ago. I could never pay him back
> for what he did. I've no family and I've been look-
> ing for someone to have these. You seemed right
> interested the other day. Mind, you should have
> a medal really for what you've done. All our love,
> Alfred Furness and Queenie

Sometimes, there are no words . . .

Kathie and I worked hard to clean up the swan in the garage and soon she was looking good – as near normal as we could get her anyway. We accumulated a small mountain of soft sponges, old towels and rubber gloves along the way. Taking care to stroke feathers only along the shafts towards their tips and avoiding damage to the flight and tail feathers had made for slow progress. Our success, though, had left us with yet another problem. The bird's feathers had lost all their natural oil during the cleaning process and she needed time somewhere to recuperate and get herself in better condition. The garage was already looking the worse for wear and we couldn't give her the time and attention she deserved. I asked around and it was my old mate Jeff Knowles in Bury who came through for me this time. He said he had a Polish lady with an absolutely impossible name who ran a bird sanctuary in his patch and he'd ask her if she could help. A few days later we were on our way to Radcliffe and the sanctuary.

I was impressed by the place and the lady with the impossible name and left the swan in her care. Later, Jeff and I released the bird at a suitable, secret location and it was another job well done. The buzz from seeing her sailing regally away across the water was indescribable, so I'm not going to try. But it really did make my day.

It was the next week that I called at an address off Whalley Road, Clayton-le-Moors, on a routine complaint. The caller was concerned about a dog with an overgrown coat that was rarely, if ever, groomed. There was no reply at the front door but I could hear the dog barking inside. I tried the rear of the terraced property and found the back gate was open – my lucky day. Peering through the kitchen window I saw what looked to be an old English sheepdog with a grossly overgrown coat. The neglect involved was considerable and I decided this might be a case for prosecution. I couldn't immediately remove the dog so I got on with other work and called back several times, hoping the owners might have returned home. About 3 p.m. I got lucky again.

A tall, smart young woman in a blue blouse and pencil skirt answered the door. I introduced myself and asked if the dog in the kitchen was hers. She told me he was originally owned by her husband but they'd separated and she'd looked after him since. The poor dog – you couldn't see his eyes at all and it must have been difficult, if not painful, for him to relieve himself, so tangled and matted was the fur at his rear end. After a few more questions I officially cautioned her and told her I was taking the dog to a vet for urgent examination and treatment. If she'd protested I'd have called a bobby who could have seized the animal by law. The police have the power to do so though an RSPCA inspector, surprisingly perhaps, does not. Fortunately, the owner was cooperative in this case and I hurried off to Halfords surgery in Blackburn where old Henry Halford examined the dog, whose name was Buster, in a vacant consultation room.

'Old English sheepdog about six years old, Henry,' I informed him. 'The couple have split up and the wife's been left with the dog and neglected him. Whether it's spite, as he belonged to the husband originally, I don't know, but look at him.' Henry was as amazed as I was and spoke in sombre fashion when he'd finished his examination.

'I have never, in all my time in practice, seen a dog's coat as tangled and matted as this chap's. There's nothing for it. We shall just have to shave off the whole mess. It may take some time. Give me a ring tomorrow afternoon.'

I was intending to go back and formally interview Buster's owner but I decided to wait till I'd checked with Henry the next day. I was pretty certain he'd support a prosecution, but by then I'd learned not to assume anything and it was best to hold fire. When I rang Halfords the following day Henry asked me to call in at the surgery later on which, intrigued by his secretive manner, I did. He was smiling when he greeted me in his rather cluttered and untidy office.

'Come in, Steve.'

'What's up, Henry? I can tell something is.'

'Not exactly. But take a look at your old English sheepdog. Rita, one of the nurses, is on her way up with him now.'

'Did you manage to sort him out all right?'

'Certainly,' said Henry knowingly. 'Ah . . .' There was a knock on the door and in marched the lovely Rita (who, in another time and place, could have been the inspiration for McCartney's traffic warden on the Sgt. Pepper album) with the new Buster – at least I had been told it was him. To be honest, I found it difficult to believe. Henry was laughing triumphantly – fit to drop in fact.

'There's your old English sheepdog, Steve . . . only he's a standard poodle!' I'd had all the stuffing knocked out of me at the transformation. It was like some brilliant magician's trick – scruffy, matted old English sheepdog, puff of smoke, and there's a shaven standard poodle. Another veterinary nurse arrived carrying two large plastic bags bulging with the matted coat Buster had been encased in for so long.

'I'd never have credited it!' I exclaimed.

'An amazing transformation, I think you'll agree,' said Henry.

'Truly amazing!' I echoed. 'But still a case, Henry?'

He looked thoughtful, carefully weighing his options. 'No. I'm not supporting a prosecution on this occasion. Why? Well; look at the dog's bodily condition. He's actually in good order. The owner may have neglected his coat but she's fed him all right. We've checked him over in other respects and he's in good health too. I'd recommend a monition – that written warning from headquarters – or a severe caution.'

I went away from the vets in a daze. Despite what Henry had said, I couldn't agree with his verdict on Buster. To my mind, neglect of a dog's coat on that scale and to that extent is a court case and always will be. Still, without the support of an expert witness, namely Henry, there was no possibility of the matter reaching court. What I might think counted for nothing and I could only operate within the rules and restrictions of the law of the land. When folk criticize, saying 'Nothing's been done' or 'Why hasn't that animal been taken away by the RSPCA', it's something they might care to bear in mind. Despite my occasional criticisms during this chronicle, I firmly believe that the Society's heart is in the right place and that it is an organization worthy of the public's trust and continuing support.

When I went back to see Buster's owner I cautioned her against neglecting his coat again and made sure that she understood how close to prosecution she'd been. After some little persuasion, she agreed to sign the dog over to the Society, which was an excellent outcome, and Sylvia and co. at the shelter found him a caring new home in no time at all. It helped that he was one of the few pedigree dogs up for adoption, as they always attract a lot of attention.

The next day I was enjoying a walk through the forest and along the river at Dinkley, near Ribchester, looking for . . . well, nothing really. I was off duty and sampling the superb Lancashire countryside. It was approaching lunchtime and I sat down on an overhanging rock on the wide riverbank, emptied my backpack and looked across at the fast-flowing water as I enjoyed my sandwiches and coffee.

I remembered a phone conversation I'd had with Marvin recently. He was passionate about the job too and it made me examine my own motivation more deeply than before. For me, it was the fact that you could make a difference. That difference, literally, could be life or death for an animal. Also, unlike many other jobs and professions, mine allowed me to see the results of my efforts on an almost daily basis. I recall talking to a wise old superintendent who was with me on a job very early on. He said, 'If you walk away or don't do your job properly the animal concerned will be abandoned to its fate. There is no one else. Never turn your back on your bounden duty.' I never forgot that.

They can't thank you. Often, your reward is a scratch or a bite and a visit to the A&E department of your local hospital. They'll more often than not resist your efforts to help and sometimes fight against you, but that's just the way it is. Still, if you've anything about you, helping the helpless is a privilege. I looked to the future with tremendous optimism in those early years as an inspector. It was quite something to know that, every day, I could make that all-important difference.